published by

history of ANCIENT OLYMPIC GAMES

by Lynn and Gray Poole

IVAN OBOLENSKY, INC. New York

hours with us in the ruins of the Olympic sanctuary, and made available for our study and camera, material and objects from the Museum. The contribution of Mr. Yalouris and Mr. Tzedakis to our research is immeasurable.

Dr. Henry S. Robinson, Director of the American School of Classical Studies in Athens, made history come alive for us at the American School's digs in Corinth. We shall be forever grateful that we saw ancient Corinth with Dr. Robinson, whose enthusiasm is infectious.

The people of the modern town of Olympia warmed us with the glow of their hospitality and friendliness; though unnamed here, they shall be long remembered. For our introduction to them, and to others of the region, we are indebted to Patroklos Iliades, friend and shepherd of our trek through the Peloponnese.

While we were in Olympia the days were sunlit, the nights brightened by a full moon, the very beacon that once determined the date of the Games. We choose to think that Helios and Selene provided the brilliant sun and full moon so we might absorb the very essence and spirit of the ancient Olympics.

LYNN and GRAY POOLE

Baltimore, Maryland, 1963

Τόδε τό βιβλίον ἀφιεροῦμεν

Edward J. Dziczkowski

Ος τύχα μὲν δαίμονος, ἀνορέας δ᾽ οὐκ ἀμπλακών——Pindar

BOOKS BY LYNN and GRAY POOLE

Olympic Games of Greece
Weird and Wonderful Ants
Deep in Caves and Caverns
Scientists Who Work Outdoors
Scientists Who Changed the World
Volcanoes in Action
Carbon-14
Danger! Icebergs Ahead!
Insect-Eating Plants
Balloons Fly High

BOOKS BY LYNN POOLE

Frontiers of Science
Ballooning in the Space Age
Diving for Science
Science the Super Sleuth
Your Trip Into Space
Science Via Television
Today's Science and You

ΕΥΧΑΡΙΣΤΩ

Εὐχαριστῶ πολύ . . . . sincere thanks to many classicists, archaeologists, historians, museum curators and athletic coaches who aided us in the preparation of this book.

It could never have been written without the influence of three men to whom Lynn Poole wishes to pay posthumous tribute: Dr. Louis Lord, Professor of Greek at Oberlin College, who initially sparked his interest in ancient Greece; Dr. Lacey D. Caskey, Curator of Antiquities of the Boston Museum of Fine Arts, and Mr. Francis Henry Taylor, Director of the Worcester Art Museum, whose encouragement and sponsorship were invaluable to him, professionally.

His gratitude goes to Miss Gisela M.A. Richter, former Curator of Greek Antiquities of the Metropolitan Museum of Art; Dr. Thomas Munro, Professor of Art at Western

Reserve University and Director of Education at the Cleveland Museum of Art; and Dr. Dorothy Kent Hill of the Walters Art Gallery in Baltimore, who, over a period of years, patiently answered many questions and shared their knowledge and research techniques, making possible continuing studies of Greek history, myths and mores.

While preparing and writing this book, we received enthusiastic guidance from two professors at The Johns Hopkins University, Dr. John H. Young, the W.H. Collins Vickers Professor of Archaeology, and Dr. James W. Poultney, Professor of Classics, who gave generously of their time in interpreting information that seemed obscure. Mr. Marshall S. Turner, Jr., Director of Physical Education at Johns Hopkins gave valuable assistance in having young athletes demonstrate modern methods of performing track events that could be contrasted with ancient Greek methods of performing the same sports.

Many curators gave permission for use of photographs of objects in their collections, and we do thank them for their co-operation, and give credit with the respective photographs. Those photographs for which there are no credit lines were taken by the authors with a MINOX B camera, using ASA-25 film.

In Greece, we were overwhelmed with hospitality and by the flow of information and guidance from busy authorities whose advice we sought. We had the good fortune to be counseled by the eminent scholar and distinguished author, Nicholas Yalouris, Director of the Museum of Olympia and Superintendent of Antiquities for the Western Peloponnese. Mr. Yalouris as graciously agreed to read the book in manuscript as he put at our disposal the objects and staff of his Museum. His assistant, Yannis Tzedakis, spent

CONTENTS

LIST OF ILLUSTRATIONS

VICTORY AT OLYMPIA

TIME: August 14, 448 B.C.   PLACE: Olympia, Greece

August sun beats down on twenty thousand men standing shoulder to shoulder on the grassy slopes of the stadium. The second day of the 83rd Olympic Games is about to reach its climax.

Excitement mounts as the time for the start of the *stade* race comes nearer. The Hill of Kronos, north of the stadium, makes a green background for the kaleidoscope of shimmering colors which is the moving, jostling mass of men. Deep purple garments cover the brawny shoulders of merchants from Asia Minor; bright blue cloaks fall in

·1

graceful folds over the sleek bodies of citizens from Aegean islands; robes of saffron yellow are worn by sunburned pioneers from a new Greek colony in Egypt. Brilliant hues are accented by the pure white robes of Athenians in the crowd.

Searing sunlight, showering on the valley of Olympia, fails to wilt the enthusiam of this crowd. Absent-mindedly, and without complaint, men, dripping with sweat, slake their thirst with cool water gulped from upended clay jars or scooped by the handfuls from the marble trough lining the race course.

A catch of breath by every man near the entrance contributes to the giant-sized sigh which spreads over the stadium before dwindling to silence. The judges are here!

Purple-robed, the judges stride toward the southeast corner of the arena, there to take their places in the stadium's only seats. Every head turns from the judges at the first strident notes, loud and insistent, blown by heralds standing at the western end of the arena. The competitors are on their way!

Cheering swells as the twenty racers emerge from the Sanctuary of Zeus into the stadium.

The slanted sunrays of late afternoon strike the naked bodies, gleaming with oil and reflecting the light like twenty mirrors of polished bronze. The athletes, proud chins lifted high, advance with lean and taut muscles rippling through their racers' thighs.

Ears hurt from the crescendo of sound. Fortunately the maddening volume decreases so the herald can be heard as he calls the name of each contestant, his father, and the city represented. Loud applause for "Leonidas, son of Kimon, honored citizen of Thebes," and for the other nineteen racers.

The line of contestants veers sharp right toward the starting line, a series of grooved stone slabs set into the ground. Olympic officials order the formation of a circle and, there, talk earnestly to the runners. Final instructions for the event. On signal the circle breaks up with exuberant gestures and shouts from the contestants. Each prepares for the *stade* in his own way. A dash down the race course and sprint back to the starting line. A squat to the ground and a leap into the air. Circling in one place fast, and ever faster. These preparations, expertly executed, are the warm-up of muscles for the final effort toward the coveted win.

A trumpet call shrills, and silence hangs on its last note. This is the awaited moment.

The racers reach their assigned positions between upright posts set along the starting line. Twenty pairs of feet grip the grooves with tense toes. Twenty supple bodies bend slightly.

A second trumpet note pierces through the stadium.

Twenty thousand spectators hold their breath. Twenty racers crouch low. Two hundred toes dig deeper into the starting grooves.

On the official signal the runners start. They're off!

Separate calls of encouragement, entreaties from bettors, cheers from athletes defeated earlier by these twenty runners, blend into a mighty din.

Oblivious to the uncontrolled yelling, the runners speed down the 200-yard course. Arms held close to the body alternate back and forth, forward to rear; legs repeat the pattern. Swift motion makes a blur of the bulge of biceps, the muscle-tightening of buttocks, thigh, and calf.

The *stade* race, just started, is almost over. The racers are so well matched they seem to be twenty abreast. Can they finish in such close formation?

Three racers suddenly put on bursts of speed that seem impossible. Barely foot-touching the ground, the three flash over the finish line. Which of the three is the winner? Epialtes of Rhodes? Diomedes of Athens? Cleonoumos of Sparta?

No one here among the spectators envies those who must make the decision. The judges, their eyes on the racers, watch intently until the last one crosses the line.

There is no consultation among the judges. Each man makes his own decision by himself. Which of the three racers, who seemed to cross the line as one, should be singled out as winner? Did one lean too far forward at the start? Did another falter on the course? Or show an ungainly gait? Rhythm of the race must be considered. The form and grace of the contestant count as much as crossing the finish line first.

Having slowed to a turn after the race, the runners trot back and forth, cooling down and relaxing muscles. They show no impatience with the delay in the decision.

It is the spectators who are restless. Those with wagers on Epialtes, Diomedes and Cleonoumos pummel each other, gyrate with glee, slap backs; each is sure that his racer is the winner.

Five minutes pass. Ten. The quarter of an hour seems so long a time to deliberate. Tension mounts. The judges turn toward each other. The decision is being made. Each judge casts his secret vote.

A herald, summoned by the judges, steps forward. A hush sweeps absolute stillness over the stadium. The three potential victors stand like statues.

The herald takes his place in the center of the race course. No one needs to strain to hear the clearly enunciated words, "Diomedes, son of Xenocrates, honored citizen of Athens, come forward!"

Wild olive tree at Olympia.

Diomedes, judged winner, is an Olympic champion!

And, like a champion, Diomedes walks toward the judges. No emotion of pride, joy or happiness crosses his strong face. At the judges' table, he halts, calm and erect. From the table, one of the judges lifts the crown, the crown of wild olive cut from a tree with the gold sword of a stalwart youth of pure Greek parentage.

Bowing his head slightly—no Greek kneels to friend or foe—Diomedes feels the crown curve on his brow. The champion's family, friends and devotees, swarming from the sloping banks of the stadium, engulf Diomedes. He is lifted to the shoulders of his brothers who carry him in naked triumph down the 200-yard course. Even friends of the losers throw garlands and bunches of flowers to the new Olympic victor, hailed by all.

"*Xaírete!*—Rejoice!" The word echoes through the valley of Olympia.

Yonder is Xenocrates, father of Diomedes, beaming at his son. And no wonder. Twenty years ago at another Olympic Games, Xenocrates himself was victor in the *stade* race, this same event his son has just won!

Look at the body of Xenocrates, stripped quickly now, as he joins the victory march. The cheer from the spectators for the fine physique of the forty-year-old father has in it admiration but no tone of surprise. After all, every Greek is supposed to keep fit by daily workouts at a gymnasium.

Megakles, blood-given friend of Diomedes, is not one of the well-wishers crushing around the victor. It is known that Megakles was given the honor of carrying the news to Athens, if Diomedes won. As the herald's announcement left his lips, Megakles dashed from the stadium according to plan. A youth of fine-drawn figure, he sped across the Sanctuary, and down through the valley to a waiting chariot drawn by four white horses.

Three days hence, Athens will be prepared for the triumphal homecoming of her Olympic champion. Plans for the celebration will get under way as soon as Megakles arrives in Athens with the great news. Pheidias, greatest sculptor of this time, may delay work on the Acropolis sculptures to begin his statue of the victor, the long-limbed son of Athens. Pindar will write a Victory Ode to be sung by the fairest girls and the handsomest youths in honor of Diomedes.

At Olympia on this afternoon of triumph, Diomedes is now carried to the altar of Athena. The crowd following him is quiet. The victor's body arches in a graceful curve as he vaults from the shoulders of his father and brothers. Solemnly, Diomedes approaches the altar of Athena, patron goddess of Athens, his home city many miles away. He sacrifices a pig in thanks to the goddess for conferring on him the highest honor a Greek can achieve.

While Diomedes and his friends go to the gymnasium where the victor showers and dresses, Xenocrates hastens away to give orders for a banquet in his son's honor.

At the Athenian camp site high on a hill across the Alpheos River, colorful tents glow against deep green cypress trees brightened by the sunset. Many servants prepare the feast.

Two by two or in groups, friends from neighboring camps stroll to the banquet. Each guest is handed a handsomely painted *kylix,* a shallow round cup, filled with wine from Attica. Spilling a few drops from his *kylix* to the ground in honor of the gods, each guest in turn proposes a toast to the champion, now smiling and relaxed. Diomedes is indeed worthy of the toasts which praise his athletic ability and victory; his beauty and goodness; his valor and courage.

At nightfall, bonfires flare brightly from the many camp sites at Olympia. No flames shoot higher or burn brighter than those from the fires at the Athenian encampment. The banquet is magnificent. Revelry, music, and songs accompany the celebration of feasting and dancing.

It will be long after midnight before silence settles over Olympia—a name which for centuries to come is to stand as the symbol of sportsmanship and fair play.

BEAUTIFUL AND GOOD

Beauty to the Greeks was the very essence of virility. Athletics, music, art, and literature were given places of equal prominence in education. From childhood every Greek boy was taught athletics because a finely formed body was of major importance; and he learned to appreciate the arts and literature because it was essential to have a well-developed mind. The perfect balance of mind and body followed the ancient Greek belief in *meden agan,* which means "nothing in excess."

*Kalòs k'agathós—the beautiful and good—*was the touchstone and secret of the pre-eminence of ancient Greece for more than 500 years. *Kalòs k'agathós* was the spirit of the ancient Olympic Games in the peak centuries of their history.

Greeks so revered beauty that it was to them synonymous with goodness. Plato expressed the Greek credo with a classic line, "From the love of the beautiful comes every good thing in heaven and earth." In his *Republic,* he stated that "virtue will be a kind of health and beauty and good habit of the soul, as vice will be a disease and deformity of the soul." Sokrates reminded his pupils that *kalòs k'agathós* is the mark of every vigorous man; the mark of any gentleman worthy to be called Greek. The philosopher stressed that constant striving through body and mind for the state of *kalòs k'agathós* must be the goal of every man.

The great Perikles, statesman, general, and athlete, said that men seeking the harmonious development of body and mind should "work for the perfect beauty of our bodies and the manly virtues of our soul." In a famous funeral oration to the Athenians, he said that "we are lovers of beauty without having lost the taste for simplicity, and lovers of wisdom without loss of manly vigor."

No man or boy of ancient Greece was ashamed to admit to a consuming interest in things beautiful. Emphasis on well-rounded training of mind and body created a culture and a way of life that influenced subsequent civilizations down to our very own. The ideals of *kalòs k'agathós* and *meden agan* produced generations of Greeks who trained from boyhood to use their minds and bodies for the cause of the beautiful and the good. Outstanding proof of the supremacy of ancient Greeks in the creative arts can be found in the following list of men who lived in the fifth century B.C.: The statesmen, Perikles and Themistokles;

the dramatists, Aeschylus, Euripides and Sophokles; the sculptors, Pheidias and Polykleitos; the architects, Iktinus and Callikrates; the poet, Pindar; the philosopher, Sokrates; and the historians, Herodotus and Thucidydes. Titans all, these men believed in *kalòs k'agathós*.

Instinctively the Greeks realized that all men might fully appreciate beauty only by participating in the arts. With complete naturalness, boys painted, carved in stone, learned to play the flute and the lyre, to sing and to dance.

Dancing was a form of athletics and, as such, was used to strengthen and tone up the body. Dances were strenuous and often warlike; one of the most famous was the *Pyrrhic Dance* in which the performers, carrying war shields on their arms, were accompanied by melodic flutes and clanging cymbals. Beauty, grace, suppleness and control learned through dancing aided men in the execution of athletic feats. The Greeks considered the dance to be an expression

Pyrrhic Dance with bronze shields, performed by young men as part of artistic and gymnastic training.

Akropolis Museum, Athens

of virility. It has not always been a symbol of manliness but scientific tests of the twentieth century prove that a dancer performing a full-length ballet uses more energy and physical force than a fullback playing an entire football game.

The Greek male exercised nude and wore no clothes in athletic events. It was manly and normal to take pleasure and pride in observing and praising the nude physiques of athletes. A spectator had no fear of a slur on his masculinity if he commented, "*Kalos pais*—the boy is fair," about a nude male in action. Physicians learned about anatomy from observation of athletes in action. Sculptors reproduced

British Museum

Pot-bellied, obese boy ridiculed and taunted by athletes in gymnasium.

in magnificent statues the nude athletes they had watched in competition.

The Greek who let his body slump and become misshapen was a disgrace. The pot-bellied male, rare in ancient

Greece, was an object of ridicule and scorn as is shown in a fifth century B.C. vase painting.

The Greeks thought that the Persians, the Egyptians and the Scythians were effeminate because they hid under-developed bodies beneath flowing robes, and walked with mincing steps in a perpetual mist of perfume.

The Persian king, Darius, for his part, misguidedly decided that the Greeks were an inferior race. Determined to conquer the Greeks, Darius sent a spy to report on how the enemy trained for battle. Disguised as a merchant, the spy infiltrated the ranks of the Greek army. He observed Greek soldiers practicing athletics, their oiled and naked bodies flashing in the sun; dancing, clad only in a bronze shield; walking arm in arm, hand in hand. He listened to poets reading aloud to strong-bodied soldiers, sitting at rapt attention. The spy returned to Darius and reported that the Greeks spent their time prancing around in the nude or sitting, partially clothed, while listening to idiots propound ridiculous ideas about freedom and equality for the individual citizen.

Darius, sumptuously garbed in luxurious robes, and his courtiers, silk-draped, guffawed at every word of the report. What an easy job it would be to conquer the decadent Greeks! But laughter turned to terror when the Persian army was driven out to sea at the Battle of Marathon. Darius could not comprehend the source of Greek strength.

Nor could his son, Xerxes, who later tried to conquer Greece. Word came to him the night before his naval forces were to engage the Greeks at Salamis that Themistokles, aboard his flagship, was in serious discussion about the relative merits of certain words used in a Pindar ode. Xerxes snickered. The next day he wept when he saw his naval forces routed by "the art-loving Greeks whose only weapons are their virile bodies and steel minds."

Darius, Xerxes and other despots, before and after them, felt the power of Greek physical and mental superiority.

From the age of seven, every Greek boy attended school where he read the epic poems of Homer and recited passages from other poetic works that inculcated the highest ideals of life. Each boy was encouraged to think, to argue with his teachers, to use his mind creatively; it was not enough to learn facts and dates for recitation by rote. The same students were taught to sing and dance, to draw and paint. Their athletic exercises were designed to toughen young physiques, to develop muscles, to increase grace of movement.

When youngsters became *epheboi,* older teen-agers, they were given advanced instruction by *paidotribes,* trainers, who taught the rudiments and rules of boxing, wrestling, running, jumping, throwing the javelin and the discus, dancing and chariot racing. Since grace and style were important to an eventual victory in competition, the *paidotribes* employed musicians to accompany participants in most of the sports. Paintings from Greek vases and passages from Greek literature disabuse any idea that *paidotribes* were mild-mannered; they were in fact stern taskmasters of the whip. Any youth caught in faulty execution of a sport or dancing felt the cut of the trainer's whipstick used with speed and precision.

The *epheboi* and men of a community convened for athletics in the *palaestra,* the gymnasium, or the stadium. The *palaestra* primarily was a wrestling school. Almost every city had its public *palaestra* paid for with public funds and built in juxtaposition with a larger building, a gymnasium, a Greek word meaning *an exercise for which you strip naked.* At some *palaestras,* owned by *paidotribes,* young athletes paid money for their training.

The *palaestra* was a square building closed on four sides by marble walls, with an inside portico, columned and covered, along the four walls. Opening from the portico were rooms where athletes, young and older, disrobed and oiled their bodies from jars they brought with them. When the *epheboi* were oiled, they went into the center of the *palaestra,* which was open to the sky. In the center courtyard, they learned the fine points of all sports from the stern *paidotribes.*

British Museum

In the gymnasium, young man having ankle massaged by servant; youth pouring oil from flask to oil his body; young man folding his cloak in preparation for anointing body in advance of exercise.

The gymnasium, though rectangular in shape and larger than the *palaestra,* was similar in architectural design: with covered interior portico and open-to-the-sky courtyard, and rooms for disrobing, oiling, body-powdering to keep the skin cool, and for bathing after exercise.

Following the practice of sports, the foot races, and boxing matches, athletes scraped their bodies with *strygils.* The *strygil,* a piece of bronze curved to fit around the arms, legs, torso, and buttocks, scraped off oil, powder, and sand from the practice arena. Then the athletes used beautifully designed vases to scoop water from large troughs with which most gymnasiums were equipped; the athletes showered each other with the water vases. At more elaborate gymnasiums, there were shower baths with water, piped from outside, gushing from animal heads, fashioned from fine-wrought bronze. Records from ancient Greece indicate that there was as much horseplay in shower and dressing rooms

Athletes bathing after exercises as they discuss the merits of each other's performance in the gymnasium.

British Museum

as there is in today's locker rooms. Water fights were common. Towels were flicked at bare buttocks with snap and sting. Human nature seems not to have changed in that respect.

The stadium, usually with earth embankments for spectators, was for track events. The simple straightaway track had a starting line at one end, the finish line opposite; the lines were stone sills set in the ground, and their design varied with the stadium. On the stadium track, athletes competed in running races, the discus throw, and hurling the javelin; in free-for-all *pankration,* a combination of boxing and wrestling. The stadium, the arena for athletic festivals and competitions, had to be large enough to hold throngs of spectators. The stadium at Olympia accommodated 20,000; later the embankments were raised to hold 40,000.

The athletic area of the *palaestra* and gymnasium, and sometimes the stadium as well, was the social center of the city, the town, the community. Early each afternoon the *epheboi* and the men left their homes and the market place to converge on the athletic grounds. Conversation was as much a part of the activities as sports. There was discussion of philosophy, drama, and poetry, of the sculptors' latest work, of politics and local affairs. The *epheboi* took their training with the *paidotribes*; the older citizens perfected the skill of their own special sport, or practiced another.

Athens, the largest city in Greece, had three athletic areas: the Academia, the Lyceum and the Cynosarges, each with an adjacent olive grove for shady walks and spirited talks. Athletic training and competition periodically were accelerated as every *epheboi* and adult athlete strove to do better than best in individual effort. Each hoped to be chosen to represent his city in one of the famous four festivals where the best of athletes from each Greek city met to contend with each other. The four Games were the Nemean, Pythian, Isthmian, and Olympic.

VALLEY OF OLYMPIA

Greece is an exciting land of rocky valleys separated by long-pronged fingers of rugged mountains, running from north to south. Barren mountains with sparse vegetation divide villages where for thousands of years the proud Greeks have toiled to wrest a simple living from unco-operative soil. Over this monochromatic landscape, an all-pervading, brilliant light and crystal-clear air create a cease-less shift of color, producing a lustrous polychromatic cast.

Olympia, brightened by the fabled clear air, contrasts sharply with barren lands around it. In splendid isolation, Olympia is cradled in a verdant valley of pines and wild olive trees; a bright jade amidst the rocky hills of southwest Greece. The valley is formed by two broad rivers, the Kladeos and the Alpheos, which border a broad alluvial plain between the evergreen hills. Olympia, known to us as the birthplace of the Olympic Games, was sacred to the Greeks long before the Games were formalized.

Some ancient writers ascribe the origin of Olympic Games to peace-treaty contests dated as far back as 1100 B.C. Greeks of that era were capricious. They were overly sensitive to any slight on their local city-state status, and quick to take up arms against any encroachment on territory, or the individual freedom which Greeks prize above all else.

In the region around Olympia, there were three prominent cities: Pisa, Elis, and Sparta. The king of each was always warring with one of the others. An occasional keen-witted despot realized that it was sometimes more profitable to talk rather than to engage in bitter fight. At such a point in history, kings of the three cities used the isolated, off-limits valley of Olympia as a neutral ground, much as Switzerland has been used in modern times. The dissenters met to make peace treaties, to establish an uneasy truce. Gradually Olympia became an inviolable precinct which, according to ancient writers, "was sacred to the gods and vital to man's being."

When a group of Greeks got together they gave vent to their innate desire for fun, for sports, for competition, for betting. The Greeks were really the first people to have unrestrained fun on a big scale! So, during times of truce, Olympia served as much for a sporting ground as for settling real or imagined grievances. The finest athletes of each kingdom accompanied their lords to Olympia, and there vied with each other in all sorts of games. Even the earliest of Greeks spent most of their time developing their bodies into steel-strong mechanisms. Basically, the reason for such physical perfection was to preserve their individual and city-state freedoms from any assault. No nation, no people have been more fierce in fighting to protect their national and individual freedom than the Greeks.

They have a passionate belief in freedom. To preserve that freedom, every boy was trained from infancy in the use of his body, in military tactics. When not being used for warfare, their bodies were kept honed through athletic competition—which in turn was correlated with their sense of fun. So, the peace-treaty meeting at Olympia synthesized all elements and turned the truce gathering into a joyous athletic event.

There is no doubt that games beside the *Altis* at Olympia had their start in this manner. Nevertheless, the Greeks themselves ascribed Olympic origin to more exalted beings —the gods of Greece. One of the wonders of the Greek civilization was that, unlike all predecessors in history, the Greeks did not worship celestial bodies, natural elements, or weird animals as gods. The Greeks, unique in tumbling the fierce gods of Assyrians and Egyptians from their deified animalistic pedestals, created their own gods in the form of human beings. The gods of Greece were the first to be endowed and invested with the fun and foibles of human beings, fashioned in the magnificent bodily forms of men and women. The gods were created in the likeness of the people of Greece. Gods and men had a kinship and felt comfortable with each other. Therefore, it was only natural that any great event should be attributed to a god, or demi-god.

Pindar, a great poet of Greece, in his famous Eleventh Olympic Ode to victory, says that the Games began at the dawn of man's life on earth. He claimed the Games were started by Herakles (the Roman Hercules), son of Zeus. One day an impudent, upstart mortal named Augeas made disparaging remarks about Zeus, and so angered Herakles, the original muscle-man, that he challenged Augeas to a wrestling match. Meeting on the flat alluvial plain formed between the two rivers Kladeos and Alpheos, Herakles gave Augeas the drubbing he deserved. The wrestling match was historic! Both wrestlers "had muscles which bulged to the thickness of a man's arm," and were so strong "each could crack the neck of the strongest man." The battle raged as each threw the other, and grimaced in pain from the half nelsons and other torturous holds secured. For hours they fought until their massive muscles were strained to the utmost; until joints bid fair to be pulled from their sockets. But—Herakles, the master of all, bested his adversary, leaving him a senseless mass of quivering flesh on the ground.

After the battle, the giant Herakles walked around a large area, dragging a stick behind him. The rectangular arena marked off by the stick he called the *Altis,* a sanctuary dedicated to Zeus, the chief of all gods. Having marked off the *Altis,* Herakles decreed that a temple of finest marble should be built to honor Zeus, and should be staffed with priests the year around. Furthermore, he ordered that another building, placed to the north of the Temple of Zeus, should be called the *Prytaneion,* the priests' council house; it should contain an ever-burning fire of Hestia, the mild-mannered goddess of hearth, home, and fire, and daughter of Zeus.

Not content with heaping such honor upon his father, Herakles stated that every four years games should be held in honor of Zeus. The finest athletes with the fairest of masculine physiques should meet at Olympia for sporting events.

Walters Art Gallery, Baltimore

Herakles hoists the writhing Anteus in a death-dealing wrestling match, just as Herakles fought Augeas at Olympia in a match which mythology records as the event said to be the founding of the Olympic Games.

Like all gods, and all athletes, Herakles wished to make known to posterity his own prowess, so he ordered a fine statue to be cast in bronze and set up in the *Altis*, in commemoration of his victory over the lowly mortal, Augeas. That statue was erected, as were thousands of other statues in honor of victors at Olympia, during the golden ages of Greece.

Pindar took a poet's license with facts as he waxed eloquent about Herakles' founding of Olympic Games. Fact undoubtedly mixes with fancy in Pindar's account, as it does in the legend of Pelops.

In the most ancient of olden times, King Oenomaus was the tyrant who ruled the Olympian valley and surrounding territory. Like all fabled kings, Oenomaus had a daughter of incomparable beauty; like the others, he felt that no man was good enough for that daughter. Suitors came seeking her hand. Oenomaus had a trick of his own for disposing of these unwanted men, anxious to plight a troth with the daughter, Hippodameia. King Oenomaus, a strong athlete with agility and a superb master of the chariot race, challenged each suitor to a physical contest. The agreement was that each suitor could try to best the king-father, but should the suitor lose, he forfeited his life.

Such a challenge deterred many suitors; but there were others who so coveted the fair Hippodameia, and her father's rich kingdom, that they accepted the terms of the king. None won. All died. All died, that is, until a Phrygian prince, named Pelops, came along. He used his conniving mind as well as his magnificently trained body, accepted the king's offer, and asked that the contest be a chariot race.

In the light of the full moon in September, Pelops met the king's charioteer, Myrtilus, under the wild olive trees on the Hill of Kronos. There the dastardly Pelops offered a bag of gold to the traitorous Myrtilus if, on the next morning, the charioteer would loosen the linchpin on the king's chariot. The gold sparkled in the moonlight; the charioteer's merciless heart beat with greed; he accepted the offer of Pelops. When the sun was high the next day, Pelops and Oenomaus stepped into their chariots behind horses champing at the bit. The starting signal was given. Both men lashed their four horses. With the king's court shouting and cheering, the two men dashed down the stretch of the hippodrome at Olympia. Neck and neck the horses ran. On the first turn King Oenomaus whipped his four white horses to make the first move for the lead. As his chariot thundered around the corner, the linchpin came loose. Oenomaus, catapulted headfirst out of his chariot, was trampled by the hooves of Pelops' horses and ground to shreds by the sharp bronze wheels of Pelops' chariot.

Pelops was victor. He married Hippodameia, took over the realm, and ordered that every four years games should be held in his honor at Olympia; that a temple should be erected to honor his patron god Zeus; and that a bronze statue of himself, Pelops, should stand in the center of the *Altis*. Wishing to appear modest, unassuming, and not grasping for material things, Pelops asked that he not be given gold for his victory; instead, he requested that a branch of wild olive be placed on his head as a symbol of his victory.

Pelops' victory is shrouded in legend but many Greeks were certain that the event marked the founding of the Olympic Games. Proponents of the legend pointed to the fact that the southern half of Greece is called the *Peloponnese,* the island of Pelops. Again fact mingles with fantasy.

It is historical fact that games were played at Olympia in 884 B.C., a year when the kings of Elis, Pisa and Sparta were in the midst of one of their bickerings over boundaries.

To celebrate the meeting, they turned attention to games. Athletes from the three cities, who met in front of the altar of Zeus, swore they would compete with fairness and honor. The games continued for several days. Winners were crowned with olive wreaths. Statues were later erected to commemorate their victories.

So successful were the games of 884 B.C. that athletes and proud city officials from all over the Greek world came to Olympia. The diplomats made deals; merchants traded with each other; artisans sold goods; athletes came for the competitions. Men came from as far away as Miletus, a Greek city in Asia Minor; from the Greek island of Rhodes, a few sea miles from the coast of modern Turkey.

Gradually the political, economic and athletic meetings became formalized. Rules and regulations were set down for training and competition among athletes. A priestly class of custodians was appointed to function at Olympia throughout the calendar year, and to handle all arrangements for the Olympic Games, scheduled regularly. Olympia was not a town where people lived and worked; it was a sacred precinct set aside for truce and games.

There are no records of those early games; few facts to tell us who competed and who won. But we do know that later Greeks considered the Olympic Games of 776 B.C. to be the historical founding of the Games. Official recognition was given to the games of 776 B.C. by all the city-states. There were many events—but only one was official. This was the foot race, won by a lean-limbed, sinewy youth by the name of Coreobus. *His was the name entered on the official records as the first winner of the first official Olympic game.*

From that time on an official listing of winners was kept. The listing was so accurate as to dates that modern historians have been able to establish a precise dating of all Greek historical events from the Olympic records—records of games held every four-year period and known as an Olympiad.

Heavily muscled javelin thrower of the athletic type admired in sixth century B.C.

Terme Museum, Rome

Early in their history, the ideal of masculinity was the heavy-muscled, well-proportioned, large athlete. From their statues, vase paintings and other remains we recognize the athlete as the man with fabulous strength and bulky power.

History, poetry and art commemorate the feats of men like Titormus of Thebes whose prodigious feats are exemplified by his most famous, performed on the banks of the river Euenus. Challenged to lift a rock weighing 600 pounds, Titormus stripped off his clothing before a large crowd who appreciated and marveled at each corded muscle. Stepping into the shallow waters of the river, Titormus lifted the boulder first to his knees, then tossed it to his barrel chest, and, straining his arms, rolled the rock to his shoulders, from which he tossed the rock 20 yards to the far bank of the river. That feat is only one of many recorded about the popular athlete of Greece. Many a bet was won and lost when Titormus performed.

At Olympia, archaeologists found a block of deep-red sandstone weighing 318 pounds. On the block is carved the inscription noting the fact that with one hand Bibon of Kos tossed the block thirty-five yards. Bibon's feat was an exhibition, not a performance in official competition.

Across the Aegean Sea on the volcanic island of Santorin another stone, weighing 450 pounds, bore an inscription recording the fact that the son of Kristobulos, Eumastas, the island's favorite athlete, hurled the rock from his shoulders to a distance of thirty-one yards.

Without doubt the most famous of powerful athletes in early Greece was Milo of Croton, whose fantastic feats of power and physical co-ordination are extolled in poems and songs left to us by bards of Greece. Milo gradually built his physique from childhood, by the daily lifting of a young bull calf to his shoulders. As the bull increased in weight, so Milo increased in bulk and muscular strength. Such gradual construction of muscle is in the best traditions of modern weight lifting—beginning with small weights and progressing to heavier and heavier weights as the muscles grow thicker and stronger.

Amazing feats of strength were not confined to men; boys in early Greek centuries left records of their prowess, too. At the age of nine, young Theagenes of Thasos astounded family and friends by lifting a bronze statue from its pedestal and carrying it on his shoulders nine times around the outskirts of Thasos, his home town.

Theagenes was immediately given special training in athletics and went on to become a famous Olympic hero, winning nineteen victories at Olympia before he was twenty-eight years old. We know that he was a wrestler, runner, and discus thrower. Like most athletes he was trained as an all-round sportsman; not concentrating his efforts on any one sport. The final measure of the greatness of an athlete was based on how many sports he took part in.

We know of his skill, but do not know how fast Theagenes ran or how far he threw the discus. No time was kept at Olympia, or at other games; there are no records of how many minutes it took a man to run three miles, or how many seconds it took him to throw an opponent in wrestling. When judging winners in competition, judges based their decision on two facts: The finality of the competition. The grace with which the event was performed.

Today, the runner who crosses the finish line first is the winner. That was not always so, in Greek competition.

Crossing the finish line first was fifty per cent of the judging. But often a man who came in second was adjudged the winner because he ran with greater grace and rhythm, did not stumble or falter, performed his race with better form, and showed a more perfect and pleasing style than the racer who crossed the line first. Athletics in Greek times were a combination of firsts, farthests, fastests—and *aréte,* the Greek word for all-round *perfection* of beautiful performance.

Because of this, Greeks, from early boyhood, were drilled by stern trainers, who taught the fine points of athletics. Training was accompanied by the music of flutes that ingrained in the youths a sense of rhythm, beauty, and style.

When we watch races, jumping events, pole vaulting competitions today, it is difficult for us to understand how and why the Greeks placed such emphasis on the style and grace of performance. We approach a better understanding if we consider such modern Olympic events as gymnastics and diving for which the emphasis and point scoring of judges are based on the style of performance—*aréte.* In gymnastics the man who can do three somersaults and a flat layout on the trampoline may be judged second to the man who performs only two somersaults and a flat layout. The second competitor is awarded the win because his form, style, grace, and rhythm may be much greater than the first. He wins. The high diver who performs flashy feats may lose to a less spectacular diver whose performance is more graceful, who cuts the water cleaner than the first.

Judgment at the Olympics was based always on grace, beauty, rhythm, and style.

FROM EARLY TIMES

Ebullient spirits and a keen sense of fun; unbounded physical energy and a love of beauty made the Greeks a
pleasure-loving people—pleasure-loving with a purpose. The
inherent characteristics naturally resulted in frequent festivals where Greeks could give vent to their joy of life and
creativity. Every city and village in greater-Greece had its
annual festivals; some, like the Panathenaic Festival in
Athens, ran for several days. There were sacrifices to the
gods, readings of poetry, presentation of dramas in amphi-
theaters, dancing in the market places, athletics in the
stadiums, and general merriment everywhere.

Certain festivals gradually became specialized, notably
the festival of drama at Epidaurus and the musical festival
on the island of Delos, birthplace of Apollo, the god of
music. Other festivals were famed for athletic competition.

Of the athletic meetings, four were outstanding: They
were the Pythian Games held in Delphi every four years;

the Isthmian held every two years; the Nemean, every two years; and the Olympic, every four years.

At Delphi, the quadrennial games honored Apollo and were accompanied by a festival of plays and music in the amphitheater. In the stadium, built at the base of the high cliffs of Mt. Parnassus, contestants competed for the coveted crown of pine cut from trees in the Vale of Tempe.

The biennial Isthmian Games took place on a flat plain near the narrow neck of land which joins northern Greece with the Peloponnese. There at the Isthmus, the licentious and wicked leaders of the city of Korinth sponsored games that were honest, fair, and faithful to the sacred rules of sportsmanship. The Korinthians, who reputedly broke every moral tenet of the good life, were scrupulously moral in their athletics.

Not far from the Isthmus, to the south, was the little town of Nemea, an outstanding athletic center with fine gymnasiums, *palaestras,* and an excellent stadium. The Nemean festival, alternating with the Isthmian Games, drew large crowds and the finest athletes, who competed for a crown of parsley.

None of the other three Games ranked in importance with the Olympic Games held every four years. Olympia, the most prestigious of the four centers, became the quadrennial meeting place for the entire Greek world; the preeminent athletic center where sportsmen contended for the most coveted prize of the ancient world—the olive-wreath crown. Olympia was a force that literally unified the Greek world every four years, and exerted a tremendous control on the people. So subtle and strong was its influence that a pilgrimage to Olympia made the visitor a person of importance upon his return home. An Olympic victor was a hero for life.

No institution, no event in history has had a longer unbroken record than the Olympic Games, held continuously from 776 B.C. to A.D. 393, nearly twelve centuries. No other human event can equal that record!

Even today, Olympia exerts a magic hold over the minds of people. A visit to Olympia is an emotional, aesthetic, and intellectual experience for those fortunate enough to spend days there; an experience through which one can absorb a feeling for the hallowed ground over which the most famous people walked in the eleven historic centuries of the Greek Olympic Games. At dawn the cool sanctuary is bathed in a pink glow which gives one a feeling of exhilaration and cleanliness; a joyous reaction to make the visitor walk light as air. When the midday sun beats down on the *Altis,* sweat runs from the pores; the arena is transformed into the stark, harsh reality of what it must have been like for competitors in the blazing heat. Nights spent wandering through the Olympic grounds, with a full moon transforming the ruins into a place of deep mystery and unearthly beauty, provide a romantic transition back to antiquity.

Sitting by day in the *Altis* one can readily conjure up a vision of the peak activity which swept through the grounds every fifth year. Influential merchants and high magistrates walk and converse. Imposing *Hellenodikai* move in and out of council buildings and temples. Scholars and artists sit in the shade, discussing cultural matters, or stand in the gymnasium watching long-limbed youths at practice. Athletes exercise with dedication and concentration. All this one feels and seems to see by letting the centuries roll back to bring the past to the present in Olympia. Under sun and moon, by day and at night, the visitor is wrapped in a mantle under which is revealed the Olympia of centuries ago. The picture fades but the present-day visitor knows with certainty that Olympia, and what it stands for, is one of the places which continues to influence the entire world. Through the modern Olympic Games, Olympia lives still, though its buildings are in ruins.

Visualizing the principal structures at Olympia is essential for a complete understanding of the site of the ancient Olympic Games. A simple drawing of the layout helps to reconstruct the past.

The sanctuary lies in the alluvial valley formed by the confluence of the rivers, Kladeos and Alpheos; to the north is the wooded Hill of Kronos.

STRUCTURES AT OLYMPIA CONNECTED WITH THE GAMES

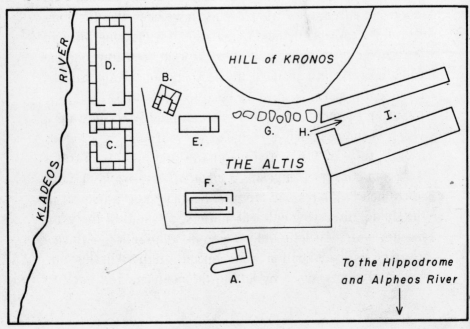

To the south is one of the most important buildings at Olympia, the *Bouleuterion* (A), the Council building. The *Boule* was the council of every city of ancient Greece; the *Bouleuterion,* the building in which the council met to carry on official business. It was, so to speak, the City Hall, the Government Office building. The *Bouleuterion* at Olympia was constructed in three parts with two elongated wings, each semicircular at the end; a square section between the wings housed the magnificent statue of Zeus Horkios, Zeus the Protector (X). On the first day of the Games, every athlete pledged to Zeus Horkios that he would compete with fairness and honesty. Members of the Council of 500, which met in the *Bouleuterion* during the games, were representatives from the cities and city-states of Greece.

Far to the north is the *Prytaneion* (B) where the *Prytaneis,* the high priests, were in residence, not only during the year of the Games, but permanently. Inside the *Prytaneion* was the ever-burning fire of Hestia, goddess of hearth and home. When sacrifices were made at Olympia, fire was taken from Hestia's hearth to ignite the sacrificial fire at any of the other altars. Priests, who tended Hestia's fire, lived and ate in the *prytaneion,* where honored guests were entertained. While the priests entertained many dignitaries, the prime function of the priests was overseeing the religious aspect of Olympia, for which every Greek had a zealous attitude. No sacrifice, no ceremony, no swearing in of judges or contestants, no treaty council could be held unless at least one of the *Prytaneis* was present.

To the west, close to the banks of the Kladeos River, are the *Palaestra* (C) and the Gymnasium (D) where athletes were privileged to exercise and take final training for the Games. Today one can wander in and out of the ruins of those buildings; and can sit where athletes disrobed, oiled and washed themselves; and walk where they practiced. It takes little imagination to invoke the feeling of the Greek athletes as they waited for participation in the events.

In the center is the Temple of Hera, wife of Zeus (E). Many of the Temple's Doric columns of rough limestone, faced with pulverized marble, stand today and give a sense of grandeur to the ruins. Hera was worshiped along with her regal husband, and in her Temple athletes supplicated for victory.

South of the Temple of Hera stands the overpowering Temple of Zeus (F). Broad steps led up to the Temple with its tall columns that supported roof and pediments. The pediments at each end were filled with majestic sculptured figures, most of which are exhibited now in the Museum of Olympia. Inside the Temple was the forty-foot heroic statue of the enthroned Zeus, created in the late fifth century B.C. by Pheidias, the sculptor of the Athenian Parthenon. The statue was chryselaphantine, gold, and ivory, with bronze accents. The left foot of Zeus rested on an elaborate footstool and, in his right hand, he held a gold and ivory statue of Athena Nike; in his left, an eagle-topped scepter.

In ancient times hundreds of statues of athletes and other famous personages were placed throughout the *Altis;* those statues were votive offerings dedicated to Zeus. Few of the statues have been found since the German School of Archaeology began its nineteenth-century excavation of Olympia.

The color, modeling, and perfection of the *Altis* statues appealed to the Roman conquerors who carried away the art treasures. Happily, a few remained at the site, and, on exhibit today at the Museum of Olympia, they give us some inkling of what a dazzling sight the entire group of fine statues must have been.

Bordering the *Altis*, to the north, are a series of Treasury Buildings (G). These buildings were not banks, holding hoards of gold; they were gems of architecture erected by city-states in honor of their patron gods. When citizens visited Olympia for the Games, they made offerings to their home-gods in the Treasury temples.

The arched tunnel (H), just outside the *Altis* to the northeast, leads to the stadium. The tunnel was reserved for priests and officials and athletes entering the Stadium (I) for the Games.

The Olympia stadium was surrounded on three sides by grass embankments where spectators stood to watch the games. The only seats, at the southeast of the stadium, were reserved for judges.

The Alpheos River long ago washed away the Olympia hippodrome for chariot races.

Women were not allowed to attend the Olympic Games. The only female present was the priestess who presided over the altar of Demeter, Mother Earth. And the eyes of the priestess were closed to the action of the Games as she chanted her prayers. The taboo against female presence at Olympia was strict; it was decreed that should a woman invade the precinct she would be immediately judged and hurled to certain destruction from the high Tymparian Rock into the death gorge below.

However, on one recorded occasion, officials relented when a woman attended the Games. She was Kallipatera from the island of Rhodes and a member of the Diagoridai family, famous for athletic and artistic achievements. She accompanied her son, Peisidorus, to Olympia where he was to compete in the boys' boxing events. Disguising herself as a trainer, the mother stole into Olympia and watched her son win the olive-wreath crown. At his victory, Kallipatera shrieked in a piercing female voice, and thereby unmasked herself. Because Kallipatera was the mother, sister, and daughter of Olympic victors, the officials had no honorable choice but to pardon her.

Olympic Games were held in the late summer or early fall after the grain harvest and the olive picking. The exact date was determined by the full moon. According to tradition, the Olympic Games were scheduled for the second or third full moon after the summer solstice, falling either in the month of *Apollonius* (August) or *Parthenos* (September). Due to the movement of the celestial bodies, the Games were held one year in August; the next time, forty-nine or fifty lunar months later, in September.

Six months before the Games, the priests and officials at Olympia sent out *spondophores,* heralds, to proclaim to all men that the Olympic truce was declared, and to announce the fixed dates for the five-day festival. From the time the *spondophores* began their truce-trek, travelers were under the protection of Almighty Zeus, the Thunderer, and could proceed with safety even through the areas infested with the most villainous robbers. Anyone who broke the truce was accountable to Zeus and to the officials at Olympia, who levied fines against truce breakers.

Powerful men bowed in submission to the rules of truce. Once, during an Olympic truce, mercenaries, working for Philip of Macedon, attacked and robbed an Athenian named Phryan. Philip personally had to go to Athens to apologize to Phryan, and to pay indemnity charges. The Olympic truce applied, not only to individuals, but to states and nations. Wars had to cease and fighting was suspended in a truce period. During the Peloponnesian Civil War, hostilities between Athens and Sparta were suspended. But, in 424 B.C., three weeks after *spondophores* carried the proclamation of truce to all cities, Sparta sent 1,000 *hoplites*, soldiers, to attack the city of Lepreum. For the action, Sparta was levied with a fine of 2,000 *minae,* a sum which the powerful city, in her arrogance, refused to pay. Her friends and foes alike were aghast at the Spartan affront to Zeus, to the Greek world, to the law of Olympic truce. Emissaries, converging on Sparta, pleaded with officials there to relent and pay the just fine. Spartans refused, so, Spartan athletes were denied participation in the Olympic Games; the official Embassy from Sparta was not admitted to the sanctuary. By the infraction, Sparta incurred "miserable disgrace in the eyes of the nations, a crime never to be erased in the minds of all men for all times."

When the *spondophores* reached a town there was celebration with banquets in honor of the forthcoming Games. When the heralds left, the city engaged in intensive athletic training that mounted as the time approached for the selection of those athletes who would represent the city at Olympia. Knowledgeable judges, appointed by the *Boule,* watched each day as the fairest and finest young men vied with each other. Finally the day of climax, long awaited, arrived: the judges announced the names of those who would contend at the Olympic Games. Hearts were broken or hearts were warmed, depending on who lost and who won the honor of competing for his city. After their selection, the nominees sacrificed each day to the gods, and intensified their training.

Every city selected an Embassy, the official group including political leaders, scholars, artists, musicians, poets, and merchants who would travel to Olympia in splendor as representatives of their city.

At Olympia, with the approach of the Games, priests and officials prepared the *Hellenodikai,* the judges for the Games, putting them through a training period. The *Hellenodikai* purged themselves of any wrongdoing, and vowed to judge each event on the merits of the individual competitors. The temples were cleaned and, if necessary, repainted. Maintenance crews worked on the stadium, the *palaestra,* the gymnasium and the hippodrome. Musicians accompanied the workmen who sang as they labored. Pressure mounted. Sacrifices were made every six hours. Excitement increased by the day. The date of the Olympic Games was approaching.

About two months before the scheduled Games, depending on the distance to be traveled, the Embassy and athletes of each city departed for Olympia. The night before departure, the city was in festival spirit. Mammoth bonfires burned bright, and the young men of the city danced around the flames. Lambs were roasted for banquets honoring the athletes; sheep were sacrificed to the gods. Revelry continued throughout the night.

At dawn the gates of the city were thrown open to

allow the exit of the colorfully arrayed Embassy and the athletes. Citizens, remaining at home, followed the procession down dusty roads for several miles and tossed garlands of flowers at the proudly erect athletes and the hopeful members of the Embassy.

Days later the travelers arrived at the city of Elis, twenty-four miles north of Olympia. Athletes and their trainers were officially presented to the Olympic officials waiting at Elis. With a formal farewell, the Embassy proceeded to Olympia.

By Olympic rules, athletes had to be at Elis for a month or six weeks before the Games started. There the competitors became acclimated to the region; spent grueling days practicing with their own stern trainers and with the trainers assigned by the Olympic Council to be sure that the athletes were at the peak of performance. Officials present made certain that "the deeds they are about to perform are in harmony with the highest moral and artistic level expected of champions." And each athlete was a champion, the best of the city he represented.

FOOT RACES

Every morning and afternoon the Olympic contestants trained in the stadium at Elis, each striving to perfect his position at the starting line by achieving the right position and balance, by toning his muscles to respond with speed to the starting signal, by correcting any minor deficiency in the grace of his stride.

Running was second nature to the fleet-footed Greeks whose major method for sending news from one place to another was by runners. Pheidippides, most celebrated of all runners, was sent from Athens to ask for Spartan aid against the military onslaught of Persian hordes invading

Greece. He covered the 150 miles between Athens and Sparta in two days—to no avail; the Spartans refused to help. Later, he ran twenty-four miles from Marathon to Athens bearing the happy news that Athenian forces alone had defeated the Persians.

It was told that, after a 400-yard sprint, Lados of Achaea, famous sprinter of his time, was supposed to have crossed the finish line many yards ahead of his competitors; his physical effort had been so great that he dropped dead after crossing the line. Later writers claim that the tale was apocryphal. The best guess is that Lados crossed the line, and continued running right on out of the stadium to his own home, many miles away, to bring the news of his victory to his fellow citizens. He was a sprinter, not a distance runner, and the cross-country run was too much for him. He died shortly after reaching home.

There's another story about Drumos of Epidaurus, a famed long-distance runner, who completed twenty-four laps of the Olympic stadium, a distance of three miles, and then, without waiting to be crowned, ran straight to Epidaurus, a distance of ninety miles, so that he himself could proclaim his victory to his family and friends. Unlike Lados, Drumos was trained to travel long distances, so he was hardly winded when he arrived home.

The stadium at Elis, used for final training of Olympic competitors, was patterned after the one at Olympia. Most Greek stadiums were approximately 200 yards long, a basic distance the Greeks called a *stade;* the English word *stadium* is derived from *stade.* Fast sprints and long-distance races were held in the stadium; there was no official cross-country event.

At either end of the stadium was a line called the *balbis,* a slab of stone set into the ground. The ancient *balbis* at Olympia, seen here with twentieth-century feet gripping the grooves, was eighteen inches wide. The two parallel grooves were seven inches apart so that one foot was ahead of the other at the start. Every four feet along the *balbis,* there was a square hole for a post which separated the runners.

Each runner remained erect for the start; they did not crouch down on toes and finger tips like modern runners. With knees slightly bent, the runner gripped the grooves with his toes and raised one heel a few inches off the ground. His tapering torso bent forward slightly and his arms thrust forward, as seen in the figurine on page 42, the runner was in an inclined position which gave him tremendous surge at the start.

Modern feet in ancient starting line for races at Olympia, showing grooves and square for posts which separated the runners from each other at start.

At Elis, preceding the Olympic Games, the runners trained at the starting line and also practiced running in loose sand. Racing over crumbly sand toughened the muscles of legs and thighs, and added power to the racers' stride, whether the contestants were preparing for the sprints or the long-distance races.

Fastest and shortest of all was the *stade* race, a distance of 200 yards down the raceway in the center of the stadium. In the *stade* the racers ran from the starting *balbis* to the opposite stone sill which was the finish line for the sprint. Next came the *diaulos,* the two-*stade* race in which runners churned their way down the raceway to the sill at the opposite end of the field, turned around the posts set in the *balbis,* and ran back to the line where they started. Each racer had to turn around the post opposite to his own at the starting line so every racer ran the exact same distance. In the two-*stade* race part of the skill was in turning around the post with skill, grace, and speed.

Vase painters, sculptors and mural painters provided us with information about the sprint. As seen here, the body

Sprinters in the one stade (200 yard) race leaping off the balls of their feet, with arms flung high.

The Metropolitan Museum of Art, Rogers Fund, 1912
14.130.12 Greek vase, amphora (123321)

of the sprinter is erect and tense; his arms are flung outward and back in swift movements to help propel himself down the track. He runs on the ball of the foot with his heels barely touching the ground at all. In swift, pounding movements his knees are raised high as his legs move with the blurring speed that we can actually see today in stroboscopic photographs.

Length of the various events in foot racing at Olympia progressed upward to the maximum of twenty-four *stades,* the three-mile distance race known as the *dolichos.* The physique of the distance runner was stockier, heavier, and bulkier, to produce both the speed and stamina needed to endure the lung-crushing punishment down and back the length of the stadium twenty-four times.

Arms for the distance race are held close to the sides, pumping rhythmically back and forth across the waist. With long, graceful strides the distance runner has his chest

Long-distance runners, jogging gracefully with long leg strides, with arms held tight to torsos.

British Museum

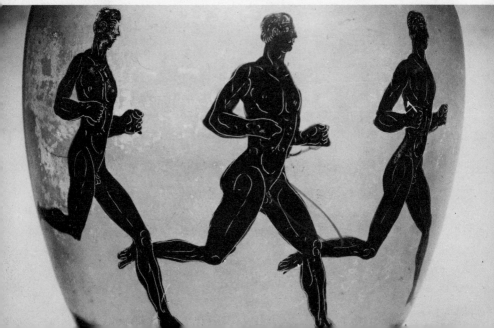

puffed out, his head erect. With toes pointed forward (one of the fine points of Greek distance racing) the runner plants his feet more flatly on the ground than the sprinter. The modern racer, looking at vase paintings from the past, is at once struck by the similarities of racing then and now.

Racing took up the better part of one day of the five-day Olympic Festival, but there was no Marathon race in ancient times. The Marathon, commemorating Pheidippides' run from Marathon to Athens, is a modern invention; it was inaugurated as a part of the Olympic events during the first modern revival in 1896.

In the fifth century B.C. a new kind of race, the armor race, was introduced into the Olympic Games. For that race, the nude runner, clad only in a heavy bronze helmet, carried a heavy bronze shield; sometimes metal greaves encased legs.

Armor exhibition race of heavily muscled men able to carry weight of bronze shield and helmet while keeping swift pace of a two-stade (400 yard) race.

British Museum

At first the armor race was an entertainment, a spectacle; then it became an official competition for racers. The racers were sturdy and powerfully muscled, with strength and endurance for a fast run carrying fifty pounds of armor. The race was a *diaulos,* a two-*stade* race down and back the distance of the stadium.

Armor races were popular with the spectators but there were not many men to participate. We know that it was a specialty event, because at Olympia the priests and officials kept twenty-five shields and helmets, all of the same weight. Having handled and lifted one of those shields on a recent visit to Olympia, we can well understand why it took a powerful man to engage in armor racing: having had on one of those helmets, we sympathize with men who raced with such accouterments!

Another popular exhibition were the torch races. These races, usually run at night, were performed as spectacles, not competitive events. In the bright of the full moon, runners, each carrying an unlighted torch, would race down the stadium to a sacred altar, plunge their torches into the sacred flame and race back to the starting line, blazing torches brightening the way.

Endless searches through the epic poems and historical writings of those who chronicled the Olympics fail to reveal any system of points by which the judges classed the competitors. Position in the starting line was by rule of stance, but how the runners were judged on points of grace, rhythm, and performance, scholars do not know: there is no detailed record. One can guess that trained judges knew exactly what to look for because, first, they had been athletes themselves, and, secondly, they had years of experience in judging. The decision each judge reached must have been based on his experience and knowledge, and finally on his own aesthetic and sensitive feeling about the individual performances. A similar method of judging performance still is used today in certain Olympic events: diving, gymnastics, ski jumping, and ice skating. Each judge assigns a certain number of points to each competitor, and an average is taken of the decisions from all judges.

A sense of frustration exists after a search for records of the speed achieved by Greek runners. Scholars find none. There was no method of keeping time; for recording how fast a famous racer could run a *stade,* or a *diaulos.* There is nothing by which to compare today's speed records with those set in the ancient Olympics.

In the final analysis, perfection—*aréte*—is an ephemeral but recognizable quality.

THE BROAD JUMP

Broad jumpers were among the most popular of athletes. Phäyllus of Melos had a following of fans which rivaled that of any modern baseball or football player. He attracted crowds of dedicated followers as did Babe Ruth in his heyday. Poets wrote paeans of praise for Phäyllus and his fine physique was molded in bronze by Polykleitus. Wherever Phäyllus went, he was trailed by a mass of admirers; both young and old felt privileged to walk near the great broad jumper. Knowing how much he was worshiped, we have no desire to be iconoclastic about this paragon of the broad jump but we must be frank in saying that modern athletes find it difficult to believe that Phäyllus did a standing broad jump of fifty-five feet. He undoubtedly was good, but not that good.

Likewise, the stories about Chionis seem to be the result of blind adulation and of abject hero worship which led his admirers to tell tall tales. He is said to have won the Olympic contest with a standing broad jump of fifty-two feet. The record is in doubt in spite of the *kalòs k'agathós* due a superb athlete.

There can be no doubt, however, that both Phäyllus and Chionis did achieve broad-jump records at least equal to if not greater than any so far achieved in recent times, for the simple reason that all Greek athletes had an aid the modern broad jumper does not have. In each of his hands the Olympic competitor carried *halteres,* stone or metal weights fashioned in various shapes. With skill and practice, the Greek could add many feet to the length of his jump by using the *halteres*, which weighed from two to ten pounds each. By their very force the *halteres* pulled the jumper forward; depending on the skill with which he handled the weights, he could arch his body forward in a graceful propulsion.

Halteres which can be seen in many museums today, were carved from stone or molded from bronze. Some had a hole by which the jumpers could get a good grip; others were cut more like dumbbells, with a small neck for grasping, and a larger scimitar-like curved section for added weight. The shape, size, and weight were a matter of individual preference; there were no rules laid down by officials.

Absence of rules about *halteres* may seem strange, and perhaps it is. But when reading the literature of the past and looking at hundreds of vase paintings illustrative of the broad jump, one comes to the conclusion that the design of *halteres* was a very personal thing. Without doubt the use of them was an individual skill, developed on general principles to permit each athlete to attain his own greatest possible distance. One man might employ a five-pound weight to jump farther than another who used a ten-pound weight. Everything depended on the style and manner in which the broad jumper swung the weight and controlled his body during the jump.

Trainers were broad jumpers who could catch the personal rhythm and style of the athlete; and like all good trainers these could help an athlete to recognize his own

Trainer with a stern stick gives instruction to broad jumper who holds halteres, jumping weights, in hands. To left of trainer is a discus hanging in its case; in the center are two javelins leaning against wall; behind athlete is a chair on which he has tossed his himation, or robe.

Boston Museum of Fine Arts

style and perfect his performance. Training consisted of four parts: The run, hop, or skip made before the jump; the take-off from the jumping line; the forward arch of the jump itself; and the firm, flat-footed landing. The Greek jumper had to land and stand erect; if he fell, he was disqualified. Since so much depended on the grace of performance, the broad jump performed by the ancient Greeks was a balletic leap of great beauty.

In the running broad jump the athlete could use a distance of about five yards for his run. *Halteres* in hand, and head turned back to get the feel of the swing, he raced forward to the *balbis*, the starting line, to make his leap.

For the standing broad jump he stood flat-footed, as shown here, swinging his *halteres* backward and forward in preparation for the second when he felt his momentum

Jumper instructed in position of halteres just before take-off. Near the athlete is a discus and two javelins, indicating that youth will take part in the pentathlon, combined competition in five events — running, jumping, wrestling, discus, and javelin throwing.

Boston Museum of Fine Arts

proper to take the leap. While getting the feel of the swing, his left foot was forward with toes pointed, his right foot was flat, his knee bent. His body leaned backward. At the precise split second of the jump his right leg snapped forward, he crouched with both knees bent and swung the *halteres* forward for the take-off.

Boston Museum of Fine Arts

Jumper showing fine form as he sails in mid-air with halteres **in outstretched arms.**

Once off the ground he swung the *halteres* forward, threw back his head, and snapped his legs up horizontal to the ground and parallel with his outstretched arms. Skilled in the control of the propelling power from his feet, legs, and thighs, the jumper catapulted forward, reaching for the greatest distance possible.

As with all jumping, part of the skill was in knowing exactly when the greatest distance had been reached, and how to handle the body at the time of landing. The Greek jumper, like the present-day athlete, practiced hundreds of times. When he neared the point of landing, he swung the

Jumper making excellent flat-footed landing, with halteres flung behind him at moment of impact. The flute player demonstrates how Greeks performed athletic exercise to accompaniment of music.

halteres behind him to add a few more inches to the jump, as well as to provide stability on landing. At this time he snapped down feet and legs, with feet flattened out to make their imprint on the sand. Then, as his feet touched ground, the jumper again swung the *halteres* forward, bringing them to a halt at his hips, an action which steadied him on landing.

Winners were selected on a combined scoring of distance, grace, and style.

Boston Museum of Fine Arts

WRESTLING AND BOXING

Wrestling is one of the oldest sports known. Art and literature abound in dramatic examples of gods and men grappling as powerful adversaries. A number of tales make a hero of Herakles, the demigod, who was reputed to have been the originator of wrestling. According to Greek myth, Herakles challenged and charged Erginus, King of Orchomenos, and their muscle-bulging struggle ended when the King was pinned to the ground. The defeat was costly to Erginus who had been extorting heavy tribute from the

57

citizens of Thebes; after Herakles outwrestled Erginus the Thebans no longer paid the tribute.

At another time, Herakles engaged in a wrestling match with a ferocious Nemean lion which had ravaged the countryside between the villages of Kleonas and Philus. Wielding his club in a first and vain attempt to strike down the lion, Herakles finally used his own bare hands to fight and strangle the beast, freeing the country people from attacks. In another myth, Herakles pitted his superhuman strength against the savage bull of King Minos of Crete; grasping the monstrous animal by the horns, the demigod wrestled until the bull was helpless.

The wrestling contests of Herakles freed human beings from forces of evil responsible for tragedy in their lives and even danger to their physical well-being. Since the ancient Greeks were emotional about good and evil influences, they may have accepted wrestling as a symbol for right against wrong, for freedom as opposed to oppression, a point of view that might have accounted for the high esteem in which the sport was originally held.

Victory was not the paramount issue in wrestling competition; the sport, like all others, had to be executed with grace, style, and skill. Each wrestler strove to attain a quality of timing and flow that produced a performance as aesthetic and beautiful as exhibitions of gymnastics and acrobatics.

Two styles of wrestling, in vogue for centuries, added variety and excitement to athletic festivals: One was known as *horthay pálay*; the other, *kúlisis*.

Horthay pálay, a free-for-all style of wrestling, was engaged in by semiprofessional athletes. Matches were fought in an area of loosened dirt, really a mud pit, where the wrestlers wallowed like animals, their bodies quickly becoming slippery with damp earth. Modern mud fights in which protagonists with bodies wet as eels slither helplessly into ludicrous positions bear no resemblance to *horthây pálay*. The bull-strong wrestlers of Greece were trained for the condition of the ground and in the technique of the sport; they grabbed opponents with clever and damaging holds in spite of the mud. There were no rounds to be stopped or started by timekeepers or referees; the match was continuous, ending only when one combatant wrestled the other to exhaustion or insensibility. With stamina and determination, typical of Greek athletes, wrestlers fought hard and long, enduring agony until one fainted or hollered the equivalent of "uncle."

Ground wrestling, like armor racing, was an exhibition event and not a competition for city festivals or the Olympic Games. Men with muscle-corded bodies wrestled for the pleasure of making their opponents plead for mercy. Spectators enjoyed the finesse and fortitude of the ground wrestlers.

Upright wrestling, *kúlisis*, beautiful to watch and requiring even more skill in execution than ground wrestling, was the accepted form of competitive wrestling. Little is known about the rules of *kúlisis*: a book of rules and a drill book assembled by *paidotribes* disappeared centuries ago. What is known about upright wrestling has been learned from the study of countless pieces of sculpture, *bas reliefs* cut in stone, and vase paintings.

After being admonished by judges that there was to be no tripping, and that no wrestler could execute a leg hold or grab his opponent below the hips, the athletes grasped each other by the wrists and leaned forward, head to opposing shoulder. From the pyramidal starting position, the wrestler advanced the left leg; his right leg, slightly bent at the knee, stretched behind with the right foot firmly planted. That stance gave him the mobility to spin on the left leg, to push forward or tilt backward on his right leg. The object of each competitor was to get his opponent off balance, and, at the same time, to be free to swing into one of innumerable positions from which to maneuver his adversary to the ground with a resounding thud.

Taut muscles of arm, leg, and shoulder etched the wrestler's frame; the muscles across the flat abdomen stood out like so many ropes. Then with the swift motion preceding an attempted throw, the wrestler's muscles relaxed in a powerful ripple throughout his body. Cheers from the spectators greeted a successful throw, counting one point for the match.

Three points were needed to win a match. A point was

National Museum, Athens

Wrestlers in standing position at start of match, with their trainer at left.

tallied if any part of the opponent's body touched the ground. If both contestants fell or the thrower slipped, touching the ground, there was no count. Frequently a three-point winner failed to be acclaimed by the spectators because he did not wrestle with the style of a champion or unattractively threw his opponent by employing graceless animal strength. A sense of aesthetics and an appreciation of skill were strong in the character of the ancients.

Many holds and techniques for throwing were permissible but examples from vase paintings and sculpture indicate that certain effective holds and throws were popular.

The neck hold was a follow-through from the pyramidal starting position. An aggressive wrestler, breaking the wrist and hand hold, grasped his opponent around the neck in an attempt to throw him off balance and then, by force, flatten him to the ground on his stomach, face down.

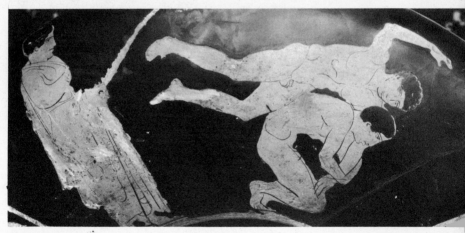

British Museum

Wrestler being tossed in the flying-mare throw; knees of thrower have not yet touched the ground; if they do, he loses the throw.

A maneuver of real beauty was the flying mare. Breaking one arm hold, the wrestler held his adversary by the other arm while, with one quick spin of his body, placing his own buttocks and back against the thighs and abdomen of the opponent. Without breaking the rhythmic motion of the body spin, the aggressor bent his body forward, dropped his knee *toward* the ground, and catapulted his helpless victim over his shoulder in a powerful swing that left the loser flat on his back. In the illustration from a vase painting, the aggressor's knees do not touch the ground. A number of the thousands of vase paintings of wrestlers show one or both knees of the challenger on the ground; and the same paintings show the judge's whipstick striking the back of the aggressor. There are no records to indicate whether there was any penalty other than the lash.

The flying mare is a graceful movement, an acrobatic feat which, even today, brings cheers and huzzahs from wrestling fans. Beautiful as is this movement, the ancient Greeks must have reacted to it with an involuntary pain in the pit of the stomach, just as we do today when we see a wrestler land with a resounding crash on his back from a flying-mare throw.

Clever wrestlers can perform a reverse of the flying mare with great success: One wrestler jerks his opponent downward from the starting hand-and-wrist grasp. Head and shoulders of the fall-man are now forced aganst the abdomen of the challenger, who quickly slips one arm across his opponent's back, as the other arm darts under and across. the abdomen. The movement allows the challenger to lock his hands under his opponent's abdomen. Squeezing the locked-in wrestler with all his might, the aggressor leans forward over the back of his pinned opponent. With strength and agility, the aggressor then leans backward; the opponent is lifted off his feet and thrown in a wide arc over the aggressor's shoulder. The unlucky fall-man lands flat on his back with the same thud as the unlucky recipient of the flying mare.

Wrestlers on this marble metope demonstrate the quick "spin and throw" technique in wrestling.

Akropolis Museum, Athens

British Museum

Wrestlers demonstrate the reverse of the flying-mare throw.

Closely allied to these movements is the spin throw. Again the challenger forces his opponent's head and shoulder down, body off balance. With one arm over the back and one arm under the waist, the challenger lifts the opponent, spinning him like a pinwheel to the ground.

The Metropolitan Museum of Art, Rogers Fund, 1916, 16.71, Greek vase, Amphora (123497)

Bulky athletes practicing the free-for-all pankration, **under eye of trainer who has a switch-stick ready for use.**

Herakles is credited with invention of another popular throw in wrestling: the body-hold-and-throw. In this maneuver the wrestler on the offensive breaks the original hand-and-wrist hold, charges his opponent until they are belly to belly. On impact, the aggressor stoops slightly and with his arms encircles his opponent just above the buttocks and lifts him off the ground. Once off the ground the defendant is off balance, but before he can do the natural thing and grasp the offensive wrestler around the neck, the challenger hooks his foot back of the knee, an action which throws the helpless man more off balance. The challenger quickly releases his grasp and in the same motion hurls his opponent to the ground. The maneuver is great, if it works; but sometimes the defendant is skillful enough to land on his feet instead of touching the ground.

In upright wrestling there were many other throws, including the cross-buttocks attack where one wrestler twisted himself around with his hard buttocks in the groin of his opponent. The position gave the challenger a chance to spin his opponent around and flatten him to the ground, if the opponent's defense is not effective.

For Olympic competition, wrestlers drew lots to determine who would wrestle in elimination rounds. Records indicate that, at Olympic Games, anywhere from six to eighteen wrestlers competed for the olive crown at Olympia. This meant that he who won the crown had to wrestle the winner of each elimination round, a feat which demanded strength and top physical condition. We can imagine that while training at Elis, before the Olympics, each wrestler and his trainer kept an eye on all other wrestlers to scout their good and bad points; their shortcomings and special skills. Perhaps one wrestler was easily thrown off his balance, another most proficient at the flying-mare throw, and another had strength but not agility. A competitor would make a mental note to take advantage of a flaw and, conversely, to guard against the special skill of another wrestler.

For centuries, upright wrestling was the only type

admitted to competition. But eventually another style, a vicious, crude type of fighting, was allowed, first as an exhibition and then as a competitive event. This was the *pankration*.

The Metropolitan Museum of Art, Rogers Fund, 1905,
06.1021.49 Greek Vase, Skyphos, (34010)

Pankrationists **battling on the ground, each wearing heavy leather thongs on hands.**
Much advice is being given by onlooker at left; at right the trainer is ready to
thwack the fighters.

The *pankration* was brutal, barbaric and bloody; it was literally a combination of the worst elements of wrestling and boxing. Beefy contestants, larded with blubber and bulk, battled each other with no holds barred; the only restriction was that fighters could not gouge each other in the eyes. They fought by kicking, biting, strangling, twisting arms, and jumping on a downed adversary; even the searingly painful, well-aimed blow of the knee to the groin was permissible. Kicking in the stomach was a favorite trick of *pankrationists*. The bout continued until one contestant was knocked out, or groveled in pain on the ground, unable to rise to continue the bloody battle.

Boxing

Greeks were as wildly enthusiastic about boxing as are contemporary devotees of the sport. But Greek boxing more nearly resembled the sport as it was practiced in the early nineteenth century than twentieth-century ring-enclosed boxing.

Tom Hyer, famous bare-knuckle fighter in America during the nineteenth century when boxing was illegal and outlawed.

Baltimore Sun

There was no measured ring or boxing area. Boxers took their position on the hard dirt in the center of the stadium and spectators gathered around, giving the boxers plenty of space in which to circle. At a command from the judges, the boxers squared off, sparred and battled until one of the contestants admitted defeat or was knocked out. There were no set rounds and no classes; the designation of boxers as welterweight, lightweight, or heavyweight is a modern device. Any Greek boxer who felt himself ready to meet any other boxer was free to enter the contests, after receiving approval of the *Hellenodikai*.

History tells us that Onomatus of Smyrna devised a set of rules for Olympic boxing but, if so, they were lost long ago. Vase paintings indicate that, whatever the rules, they were elementary. Apparently after being floored a boxer could be struck by his standing opponent. And boxers seem to have struck each other only on the head, neck, and shoulders; nowhere do we find illustrations of the body blows or hard jabs to the rib cages, so effective in modern boxing.

Boxers training in gymnasium: contestants at left (in Tom Hyer pose) have leather thongs already bound around hands and wrists; the two athletes at right are preparing to bind theirs.

British Museum

Before his match, each boxer bound soft leather thongs around his hands. On the right of this vase painting we see two young men holding the long thongs; a thong was from eight to ten feet long. A loop at the end was attached to the thumb, pulled tight and wound around the four fingers, stretched across the flat of the hand, and bound around the wrist and up the forearm. The two boxers, at the left of this drawing, have their leather thongs in place. The soft thongs were the boxer's "gloves" during the centuries when the Olympic Games were at their peak, before deterioration in amateur sportsmanship started. In later centuries, pieces of wood were added to the thongs; then spikes were set into the wood blocks; and finally, in decadent Roman times, boxers fought with *caestus,* heavy thongs bound around spiked pieces of metal.

Boxers at practice. At right one boxer has delivered a haymaker and is preparing to follow it with a knockout blow. Boxer on knee raises right arm to signal his defeat, and thereby throws in the towel.

British Museum

In the golden age of Greece, boxing was mostly a game of defense. Boxers took a widespread stance with the left leg forward and bent slightly at the knee to give spring and movement to the body, the right leg back and straight to give power for a punch or forward lunge; the left arm was outstretched to provide a guard against an opponent, the right arm bent and pulled back ready to make a lightning jab to jaw or ear. While the Greek boxer used most of the blows employed by contemporary boxers, there is no record of the ancients going into the clinch which uses up so much time and gets many a modern boxer out of a bad fix.

A study of hundreds of vase paintings shows that the Greek boxer actually used both hands for striking his opponent. His right hand delivered the swift uppercuts, the hooks, quick jabs, and feints; his left hand was used for a shattering straight blow to the chin for a knockout.

Literary works of poetry and prose praise the Olympic boxer for the sureness of movement in wearing down, then painfully stunning his adversary. Modern fans would boo and catcall Greek boxers for the slowness of the match, the repeated circling in seemingly endless revolutions; the Greeks appreciated fancy footwork and deft use of the hands in landing the final punch.

A skilled boxer's outstretched left arm was difficult to get through; the opponent had to make a swift movement to his left, get in and under the guard in the hope of landing a knockout blow with his own left hand. By the maneuver he laid himself open to a quick and often devastating jab from the right hand of his opponent.

Many of the matches of antiquity went on for hours; each contestant tried to wear the other down by defensive tactics.

One famous match, in which Diagodorous of Rhodes was finally victor, continued for six hours. Diagodorous led his opponent on, by defensive movements, drew him in and around, kept him in constant motion until the opponent fell from utter exhaustion. Such tactics might seem tedious today. The Greeks held leisurely skill in high esteem because it took stamina and special ability to wear a man down to the point of weakness that made him give up.

Eventually Greek boxing degenerated into a brutal sport with contests between charging brutes of muscular strength. Some boxers, retaining the skill and style of earlier centuries, proved that they could win over heavy lunks who battled with sheer brawn. There is an exciting account of a boxing match between the lithe and slim Polydeuces and the crude Amykus, a favorite of those who enjoyed bone-crushing sport. Amykus laughingly accepted the challenge of Polydeuces to a match that would prove which style was the best. The bout began with Amykus charging in to beat Polydeuces to a quick pulp; but when Amykus reached the spot where Polydeuces had been, Polydeuces was not there. The contest continued with Polydeuces side-stepping his opponent until the bewildered Amykus was as enraged as a taunted bull. Hour after hour the boxing match went on with Amykus becoming increasingly wild with frustration. At last Polydeuces landed a crucial blow on the jaw of Amykus, who reeled and crashed unconscious to the ground.

Style and skill won over brute force.

But brute force for hundreds of years attracted spectators in Greece. It may seem incongruous that the Greeks, sincere worshipers of the beautiful and the good, should have tolerated and even encouraged the continuance of ground wrestling, of *pankration* and boxing. That those sports survived simply proves that the Greeks were human beings like those of us living in the twentieth century. Millions of people continue to view wrestling matches and boxing bouts, screaming and yelling with the release of the brutal streak which is a part of human nature. Through recorded history man has derived satisfaction from violent sports—and the Greek was no exception.

DISCUS AND JAVELIN

Certain symbols evoke universal recognition: The *fleur-de-lis* stands for France. The flaming disc of the rising sun for Japan. Crossed red lines for the American Red Cross. The *Diskobolos* for the Olympic Games.

The *Diskobolos,* the famous Greek statue of a discus thrower sculpted by Myron, has been copied through the ages, and photographed thousands of times since the invention of the camera. The statue, shown on page 76 has become symbolic of the games of antiquity though the discus

73

throw actually was no more popular than any other sport of the Greek festivals. The discus throw did embody the ideals of Greek athletics: strength, *aréte*, physical beauty, skill, style, rhythm, and precision.

It was traditional for a discus thrower at the Olympics to present his discus to sanctuary officials after having it inscribed and dedicated to a god. While in Olympia we held an ancient discus inscribed with the words, "Kleon threw me to win the wreath." The experience inevitably was an emotional one; in our hand was the discus, symbol of the highest ideals of Greek athletics; a metal discus thrown in an event of the fifth century B.C. Standing in the stadium at Olympia, we had to curb a spontaneous, joyous urge to throw the discus into the air.

The discus of antiquity usually was fashioned from metal, though a discus made of stone was permissible for competition. Each quoit-shaped discus was tapered from the center to the thin edges, which made it easy to grasp. The *diskoi*, studied in various museums, range in diameter from eight to eleven inches; in weight from five to twelve pounds. Apparently there was no official standard for the size or weight of the discus to be used in competition. Again, as with the *halteres* for jumping, the size and weight depended on individual preference of the contestant. His discus was made to his specifications, to suit his style and technique for throwing the greatest possible distance.

Unlike today's discus competitor who throws from within a circumscribed circle, the contestant in the ancient Olympics stood inside an area called the *balbis,* marked off by three lines. The thrower could not step over the lines to either side, or across the line in front of him. Within the *balbis,* or throwing cage, he was permitted freedom; he could stand forward or to the far right or to the far left; but, if he stepped outside any one of the three lines while making his throw, he was immediately disqualified.

Statues, vase paintings, and literary descriptions of events create some confusion about the science of throwing the discus. Conflicting written statements and illustrative evidence of differences in techniques make it difficult to arrive at a clear concept of general principles. One certain fact is that the Greek discus thrower warmed up with a swinging of arms similar to the actions of a baseball pitcher. Variations in throwing methods proceed from a basic starting position: a firm stance facing the direction of throw. The athlete arched his arm and hand, moving the discus backward and forward several times and, when ready to throw, advanced his left foot straight out in front, and placed his right leg, knee bent, to the rear, the right foot on the ground.

With the discus balanced in the palm of his right hand and fingers lightly gripping the rim, the thrower swung the discus in front of him, across his chest and up toward the left side of his head. In a moment of arrested motion, his left hand met the right, steadied the discus for a split second. His eyes were focused on the discus throughout the entire swing. After the left and right hands met, the right hand and arm swung down across the chest, continued down across the hip and thigh, and on back until the right arm holding the discus was far extended to the rear of the body. Then the thrower gracefully broke the back swing and started the forward thrust. His knee-bent right leg pushed off to give added propulsion, his right arm swung forward as the right leg was thrust forward leaving the left leg back, knee bent. With his right foot planted firmly to give stability and extra power, the athlete threw the discus. A free translation into modern idiom of a Pindar comment describes the discus throw as "a pure joy to see, a harmonious symphony of ecstatic motion."

Discus thrower in moment of arrested motion when discus is at apex of backward swing, just before the forward thrust and throw.

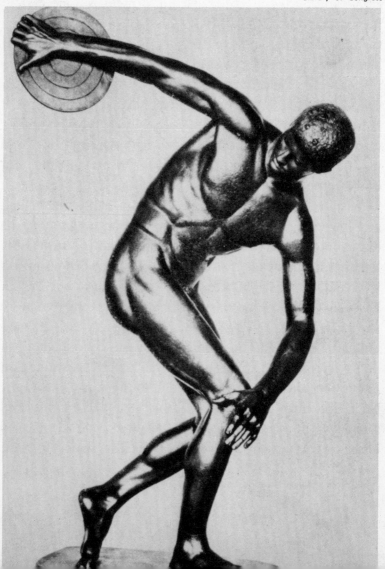

Fans of contemporary track events and specialists in today's discus throw will recognize the differences between ancient and modern styles; the ancient style was more confining, less active than the modern. We immediately note variations while watching high school, college or Olympic discus throwers in action. Sometimes the contestant stands with his back to the direction of throw; after practice swings, he pivots in a half circle toward the direction of the throw, continues to pivot another complete circle before putting the strength of arms and legs into the throw. Others, instead of making a circle and a half, prefer to face the direction of throw, completing only one 360-degree pivot before releasing the discus.

Modern discus throwers may or may not throw farther than the ancients but, imbued with the spirit of Greek artistry and grace, Robert Garrett, a young American athlete, used the ancient stance and style to win the discus throw in Athens during the first modern Olympic Games in 1896. The method was abandoned in favor of the turn-and-swing for competition. But wherever the ancient style is performed as an exhibition, it brings spontaneous applause from spectators; they instinctively recognize the grace and sweeping beauty of the ancient Greek style.

Javelin Throw

One of man's earliest skills, developed hundreds of thousands of years ago, was the hurling of some sort of spear, sharply pointed. Primitive man's spear was used for hunting animals to feed and clothe the family, and for driving off attacks from human enemies. In historic times, the Sumerians, Phoenicians, Nubians, Assyrians, and Egyptians were proficient with the spear as a device for hunting and a weapon of warfare. Throughout the Middle Ages the spear, often called a lance or javelin, continued to be useful to the hunter and the warrior. The spear became a sporting device, too. Jousting matches in medieval times were gala events with armored knights trying to unseat each other from their chain-mailed horses.

The Greeks hunted with javelins, then fought with javelin weapons, and eventually tested their skill with the javelin in athletic competition. It is believed that the Greeks were the first to use javelins for sport.

There was no deadly point on the sporting javelin; its tip

Jumper, discus thrower and two javelin throwers at practice. Javelins illustrate how the throwing thong was wrapped around the stick, and the two forefingers inserted into loop for hurling. Thong gives a spin to the javelin, as does the bore of a gun to a bullet.

British Museum

was a blunt piece of metal. Like the *halteres* and the discus, the javelin varied in size; weight and length were a matter of personal preference. In general, the javelin was about six feet long and about an inch and a half thick.

The javelin today has a wrapping of leather or nylon around the fulcrum to assure the thrower of a good grip and to prevent the javelin from slipping on a hand damp with sweat. The Greeks used a leather thong which was not permanently attached; it was approximately sixteen inches long and looped at the end. Each man wound the thong tightly around his javelin shaft, leaving the loop dangling so the middle and index fingers could be inserted into the loop for the throw. When the contestant threw the javelin, he held on to the loop; the thong unwrapped to give the javelin a forward thrust and a spin. The principle was similar to the boring on the inside of a gun barrel that gives a spin to the bullet as it is ejected.

There was no rule about where the thong should be wrapped around the shot. Each javelin thrower discovered, through practice, where thong-wrapping would give him the impetus for throwing the greatest distance. From literature we gather that many athletes preferred to have the thong back of the shaft center because such positioning gave greater spin and distance to the javelin.

In practice and competition, the thrower wound the thong tightly over the shaft, testing over and over again until he was satisfied with the security of the thong and its position. The javelin, cradled expertly in the circle formed by index finger and thumb, lay across the palm of the contestant's upturned right hand. With a stance of right leg back, left foot firmly placed in front, the contestant extended his right arm as far back as possible, right shoulder dropped so the javelin shaft pointed upward.

At the moment of throw, the athlete took a few hop-steps forward, swung his right leg forward, and put all of his precisely controlled strength into the throw. The javelin spun forward and upward, out into a graceful arc, and plummeted to the ground; soft earth sprayed from the point of impact. Judges rushed forward to put a peg in the ground where the javelin landed.

The throw did not count if the javelin landed to the far right or left of a specific sector marked for competition. And the farthest throw was not always the winning throw; as in all Greek events, grace and technique were of prime consideration. Judges voted against a throw that was ungainly or a technique employed simply to gain a few inches, just as surely as they voted against wild throws that careened or veered off beyond the measured area for competition.

Eumines of Korinth, who spun his javelin for a mark well ahead of other javelin throwers at the 82nd Olympic Games, protested an adverse decision of the judges. Eumines asked for a Council hearing but the judges there unanimously stood by their original decision, explaining that Eumines lunged in so ungainly a manner when the javelin left his hand that he was thrown off balance and fell to the ground. The performance was not up to Olympic standards; was not *aréte*. The Council not only upheld the judges but also lectured Eumines for action unseemly for an Olympic competitor.

Kalòs k'agathós influenced all aspects of athletics and life.

OLYMPIC FESTIVAL

Three days before the opening of the Olympic festival, the list of entrants was announced at Elis where the athletes had been in training for several weeks. Many disappointed would-be competitors were eliminated when they failed to measure up to the standards of Olympic officials at Elis.

The athletes chosen sometimes numbered as few as one hundred. As soon as the list was announced, preparations were made for the procession to Olympia. Elaborately robed representatives of the Council at Olympia and cer-

tain of the *Hellenodikai* went to Elis specifically to lead
the procession which began with heralds blowing their horns
and priests chanting a ritual for the assemblage. The
athletes who had survived the tests and training at Elis
marched away with their white robes, the *himations* worn
by Greek men, swinging as they moved. Some of the competitors were headed for a destiny that would make them
heroes of Greece, privileged men for the rest of their lives.

When the procession reached the village of Piera, on the
boundary of Elis and Olympia, the priests sacrificed a fat
pig to Zeus; and the athletes took part in one of the several
impressive ceremonies attendant upon Olympic competition; the one at Piera, a ceremony of purification.

Two hours from Piera, the procession crossed over a
hill and descended into the Valley of Olympia, forged the
Kladeos River, and continued past the gymnasium and the
palaestra into the *Altis*. There the athletes, officials, and
priests were greeted with thunderous cheers from spectators
assembled from all over the Greek world, mainland and
islands. However controlled in demeanor, as befitted their
status, the athletes must have experienced the chills and
shivers of personal excitement when they arrived at the
sanctuary; there the realization swept over them that they
were among the chosen, the favored few who entered the
sanctuary as competitors for Olympic honors. Deep inside,
each contestant was aware that a victory at the Olympic
festival was as great an honor as any that could be bestowed
on a Greek.

Two days remained for practice in the stadium and the
gymnasium; two days to be given over to bringing individual skill to a honed point of sharpness before the

Games began. At the 83rd Olympics, in 448 B.C., that day was August (Apollonious) 13, two days before the full of the moon.

Far into the night on August 12, bonfires flamed on the hills bordering the festival area. Friends drank and chatted in the flare from the fires but there was no singing, no celebrating, no noise. Sleeping athletes were not to be disturbed; they had to be up with the sun.

When sunrise cast long shadows across the stadium and the *Altis,* athletes and their trainers already were having the typical Greek breakfast of coarse bread dipped in wine and olive oil. After eating lightly, the participants went to the *Altis,* where the *Hellenodikai* were waiting with trainers from Elis. A herald announced the name of a contestant, who stepped forward three paces ahead of his father. Officials catechized the athlete, who answered questions about his own character, morals, and faithfulness in months of training for the events in which he was to compete at Olympia. He stood proudly alone, to give evidence also that he had full understanding of rules imposed on him by the Council. Officials cross-questioned the athlete to satisfy themselves that he would adhere to the credo of *aidos,* the gentlemanly conduct of fairness in all things. *Aidos* was synonymous with the literal meaning of everything inherent to a gentleman: courage, respect, honesty, kindliness, a feeling for beauty, and the possession of mental and physical strength.

When the athlete passed the scrutiny of officials, his father stepped forward to give proof that the contestant was a true Greek, descended from pure Greek lineage on both maternal and paternal sides of the family. Any Greek citizen, poor or rich, unknown or famous, could participate in the Games; it was required only that he be of unblemished Greek descent.

One by one the athletes stepped forward, were questioned, proved their birthright, stepped back among the other contestants. The final test passed, they were ready to participate in the Games.

Before the sun hung high at noon, still another solemn procession formed, this one near the *palaestra*. The Council members led, followed by the *Hellenodikai*, priests, contestants, trainers, fathers and other close relatives of the athletes. The procession moved past the *Prytaneion*, into the *Altis*, across the east end of the Temple of Zeus, and continued southwest to the *Bouleuterion*.

There in the Council Hall, contestants watched as priests sacrificed a pig and a sheep before the colossal statue of Zeus. Zeus, the prototype of a stern god, towered forty feet above the assemblage of men, dwarfed by the size of the statue. Zeus seemed to glower with warning at the Olympic athletes who sensed that the fury of his thunderbolts would strike any competitor failing to live up to the *aidos*. When the sacrifices had been offered, the chief *Hellenodikai* stepped forward to lecture the athletes on their duties, responsibilities, and actions during the five-day period of the Olympic Games.

As the words of warning and advice died away, the athletes in unison swore allegiance to the Greek gods, fidelity to Zeus, and solemnly vowed to participate with *aidos* of spirit and action so that no shame should come to Greece, to their home cities, or to the families whose names would be heralded to the spectators before each event. The oath of honor was followed by a similar declaration from the judges, who swore to judge each contest with fairness and honesty, with total impartiality and objectivity, and never to reveal the names of any contestants for whom they cast their vote.

With a blare of trumpets the Olympic Games were declared officially opened.

We can imagine that a resounding cheer went up from all present; that the athletes wasted no time in dashing to the *palaestra,* gymnasium, or stadium to strip off their clothing for the final practice which might add the last extra perfection of skill that would assure a victory. As each contestant worked out he was trailed by kinsmen and admirers; his style and performance were watched carefully by those who were waiting until the last minute to decide on whom they would wager heavily in the feverish few minutes of betting before each event.

Merchants, politicians, and city officials from many cities walked and talked together as they concluded agreements, renewed treaties, gossiped, and probed to gather information needed by friends at home. Good friends from far-flung regions of the Greek world talked of events and happenings of the four years since they had seen each other. Messages from those not present were delivered; sometimes arrangements were made for advantageous marriages, with dowries settled.

In the *Altis,* on the hills and along the river banks, groups gathered around famous men whose words were an education in themselves. What an assemblage there was! At the 83rd running of the Olympic Games we know that Sophokles was forty-three years old, Aeschylus was sixty-one, Euripides was only twenty-eight. No one knows whether or not these three dramatists were at Olympia at one time; they may have been because it was the place to which prominent Greeks gravitated every four years. It is known that Herodotus read passages from his history of Greece on the steps of the Temple of Zeus, and that a teen-ager named Thucydides listened with wonder and awe to the sonorous tones of Herodotus as the rhythmically beautiful classical Greek language rolled from his tongue. Thucydides himself later became the great chronicler of the ill-fated Peloponnesian Wars. During the 83rd Olympic festival the philosopher Sokrates was an energetic nineteen, already making friends and enemies faster than most men of fifty. Perhaps he too was there. Without doubt the middle-aged men of renown, Perikles, Pheidias and Iktinus, attended the 83rd Olympic Games; men of such importance would have been conspicuous by their absence. Polykleitos, the Argive sculptor, was certainly there because a victor's ode written by Pindar describes how the sculptor watched the "fair form of Menander hurl the javelin to victory." A statue of a javelin thrower by Polykleitos is one of the great statues produced in the fifth century B.C.

Late in the afternoon athletes went silently to various altars to give personal pledges and vows, to make supplications to patron gods for the strength, courage, and skill necessary to win the events in which they would compete.

Sun fell as fast as it rose over the sanctuary. Fires burned on the hills. Athletes slept. Quiet descended over the valley at the close of the first day.

Second Day

The second day of the festival was actually the first day of athletic competition. After a quick breakfast all the spectators hurried to the hippodrome to the south of the stadium. The hippodrome, four hundred yards long, ran from east to west close to the banks of the Alpheos River. Before the sun was very high, the banks surrounding the hippodrome were filled with jostling, cheering crowds making last-minute bets on the chariot which would come in first. Each owner sat in a favored place which he had staked out by having a servant sit all night at the location from which the owner could best watch the performance of his own chariot. Seldom did wealthy owners serve as their own charioteers to drive the horses in the race. Like race-horse owners of today who employ jockeys to ride the horse, Greek horse owners paid high fees to the best chari-oteers in the country to drive in the races.

With pomp and ceremony, the second day began with another great procession, as always led by officials, judges, and dignitaries for whom places had been reserved in the hippodrome. When all were seated heralds blew their blasts, signaling the chariots to pass through an arched gate into the hippodrome. Roars from twenty thousand throats floated across the valley, and echoed against the hills. As each chariot appeared, a herald announced the name of the owner, his father's name, and the city from which he came. Naturally the owner stood and took a bow for the benefit of those whose wagers were on his horses. As many as fifty-four chariots took part in one single race at Olympia; an ode to the victor of the chariot race at the 83rd Olympics, in 448 B.C., mentions forty-three chariots.

After the presentation to the judges, the charioteers wheeled their vehicles down the race course to the start-ing gate. Each chariot had his assigned place at the starting line, with the least-favored place in the center. Chariots were lined up in a V-shape, like a formation of geese in flight. The start was tricky indeed, and often brought complaints from owners. At the starting signal, chariots to the rear of the V-shape on each side moved; the chariots drew abreast of the chariots closer to the point of the V, the two sets of flanking chariots then drew abreast of the next two chariots closer to the point of the V; finally the V-shape had disappeared and all chariots were abreast of the pivotal chariot which had drawn the lot of the center-V position. By the time all chariots reached the center charioteer, his horses had to start from standing position while all others were already in full stride. To compensate for the advantage of position, all chariots had to proceed abreast for fifty yards, crossing a *balbis,* a stone sill placed in the ground, at the same time. That maneuver theoretically guaranteed a fair start.

When the chariots reached the *balbis,* pandemonium reigned. Hooves pounded like hailstones on the hard ground, whips snapped over the horses' heads, charioteers shouted at their horses urging them to greater speed. Spectators roared, screamed, and shrieked instructions—as though the charioteers could hear them in the melee! And, a melee it was. Forty-three chariots in 448 B.C. sped down the first lap, and, as they came to the first turn, there were many collisions with horses stumbling over each other, and charioteers catapulted from their vehicles.

Those still in the race made the turn at the far end of the hippodrome, rounding a center post for the return lap. Daring charioteers gambled on their own skill and the speed of their horses as the chariots careened around the center post. Some of the races were for one complete lap of the hippodrome; others, for as much as six miles, up and back twenty-four times! Without the aid of today's binoculars and motion-picture cameras, the racing judges were not always able to detect foul play and rough driving. Nevertheless, they did the best they could and often disqualified a charioteer whose actions they considered to have been rough and unwarranted.

When the dust of race settled and the judges made their decision, a herald announced the name of the winning chariot. From his seat among the other spectators, the proud owner walked forward, grasped one of the horses by the bit and led the four-horse chariot to the judges' table. There a wreath of wild olive was placed on the owner's head as he acknowledged the applause and honor, just as though he himself had run the race or acted as charioteer.

Next came the bareback races. Slender, lithe, and wiry youths were good jockeys. Owners and friends watched as each jockey, his naked body gleaming as brightly as the well-brushed coat of the horse, led his mount into the hippodrome. Again each entry was announced and the horse led to the starting line. Without the aid of a groom each jockey gracefully vaulted to the back of his horse, where he waited tensely for the start. When the signal was given the horses were off down the course, each jockey urging his horse forward and maneuvering him into a favored position to get around the post at the far end of the field.

When the horse races were over, long before noon, the crowd dashed quickly to the north, swarmed over and around the banks of the stadium for the beginning of the foot races.

Sprinters and long-distance runners had been warming up in the stadium. As the crowd filled the stadium the athletes went to the gymnasium where they put more oil on their bodies, sifted powder on the oil to close the pores, and prepared themselves for the event. On signal from an official they walked, single file, in position chosen by lot. The file passed through the *Altis* where, on the east end, they were met by the *Hellenodikai* and other dignitaries. With a blast from the heralds, the procession moved out into the sunlit stadium where the competitors were met with cheers from the crowds. Turning sharp right, the contestants lined up for identification by name, father's name, and city represented. On command, each athlete broke ranks and trotted around the stadium, jumped up and down or performed whatever exercise toned his muscles. At Olympia, twenty racers could make the start at the same time; when more than twenty entered for one race, it had to be run in heats. The heats were run on this second day of the Games, the winners each receiving an olive crown. But the main event took place on the fourth day when the winners of the first runnings met to compete for the highest honors in the sprint and long-distance racing.

In quick succession the jumpers, discus throwers, and javelin throwers paraded into the stadium for their events. Spectators hardly knew where to look: the field was like a ten-ring circus with many events. *Hellenodikai,* the judges, were assigned to each of the events, many of which took place simultaneously just as they do in modern track meets. At the end of an event, the victor strode forward to the judges' table to be crowned with the olive wreath.

Late in the afternoon the all-round athletes gathered for the *Pentathlon,* made up of five events: running, jumping, wrestling, discus throwing, and javelin throwing. Superb athletes who spent years in training for each of these events vied with others to see who excelled in all five. Only a few qualified for participation. As the sun began to sink in the western sky and drop over the hill, the *Pentathlete* was crowned. He need not have been the winner in all five events; hardly could one man, among so many magnificently trained athletes, win in each event. That would have been too much to expect. The winner was he who gained the most points for the manner in which he performed, the beauty and grace of his movements, and, also, won more of the events than any other competitor in the *Pentathlon.* To be a *Pentathlete,* the winner of the *Pentathlon,* was one of the greatest glories attained by a Greek. Winners of individual Olympic events were heroes for life—a *Pentathlete* ranked with generals, statesmen, sculptors, dramatists, and all other men of superior fame for generations to come. He was the epitome of *aréte*; of *kalòs k'agathós* of *aidos.*

After the *Pentathlon,* all athletes who had competed during the day went to the gymnasium for a bath, a rub-down, and massage for sore muscles. Then with his family, friends, and home-city officials, each winner went to the Temple, or Treasury, erected by his city to give thanks to the gods for victory. Sacrifices of pigs and sheep were made and half of each animal was sent to the *Prytaneion* to be used by the priests for Olympic feasts.

Far into the night campfires burned on the hills, men talked, dealt with each other on commercial business and political treaties; the historians read their records; poets sang their songs. Often the dawn started to creep up to turn the clouds a fleecy pink before the embers in the camp-fires actually flickered out, and men slept.

Third Day

The morning of the third day was a period anticipated by the Greeks, a people with a strong sense for dramatics; the spectacle. Parades, processions, and spectacles, especially if presented with artistry and grandeur, were (and still are) important to the Greeks.

Early in the morning people walked and talked, went to the gymnasium, *palaestra*, and stadium to watch the athletes work out. *Kalos pais* was heard repeatedly. Sculptors made sketches in clay, working with broad strokes to outline a new movement seen as an athlete performed a maneuver which the sculptor could catch at the moment when the body was actually at the apex of a motion. These move-ments can be seen today in hundreds of ancient statues; a moment of arrested motion gives the viewer a feeling of participating in the joyous execution of an athletic feat.

Mid-morning, all the judges, priests, officials of Olympia, ranking Embassy members from each city, and the athletes gathered in front of the *Prytaneion*. Spectators crowded around the *Altis*. Inside the *Prytaneion* a splendidly robed priest scooped up a pile of fiercely glowing embers from the fire of Hestia, goddess of the hearth; when he emerged from the *Prytaneion,* another priest chanted a hymn to Zeus written for the occasion by one of the great poets of Greece. Assembled dignitaries and athletes fell into line behind the priest who bore the embers aloft on a flat bowl made for this event and decorated with scenes from famous feats performed by Zeus.

Slowly the procession wended its way through the *Altis,* past the gleaming marble Treasury building, and the Temple of Hera. Respectful spectators lining the way were first silent, then vocal as they joined in the hymn of praise to Zeus. Turning south toward the Temple of Zeus, the procession formed itself outdoors around the Great Altar of Zeus. Several priests mounted the steps and lighted the fire on the altar. From a distance came the bellowing of a hundred of the strongest blooded bulls in Greece. One at a time the bulls were brought to the *Altis* and driven up the steps to the altar for slaughter; parts of the bull's body were thrown on the raging sacrificial fire, spurting grease and burning fat high into the sky. The rest of each bull's body was carried away to be roasted for the Feast of Zeus to be held that night.

Throughout the entire sacrifice hymns of praise to Zeus, and other gods, were sung and recited by poets and trained choirs. Strong men, singly or in groups, danced around the altar, much as Greek men today are inspired to dance on the spur of the moment in *tavernas,* really the social clubs of modern Greece.

When all of the one hundred bulls had been sacrificed, the procession wound its way through the *Altis,* back to the *Prytaneion.*

After a hearty lunch the Olympic visitors repaired to the stadium to watch the boxing and wrestling, and the foot racing for boys, the *epheboi* from the ages of seventeen to nineteen. Here the younger men had an opportunity to display their skill and prowess. Spectators watched these events with special interest, hoping to single out those who, four years hence, would be the best men competing in the major events of the next Olympic Games. Although events for men were major events, the boys who won were also crowned with wild olive wreaths and treated as heroes. Pindar and other poets, who wrote poems about Olympic victors, often sang the praises of the younger men whose "beautifully chiseled bodies evoked glory from Apollo, and whose promise of performance won flowers from mortals."

The night of the third day, the night of the full moon, again was given over to revelry and song, to feasting and dancing, which, according to Bacchylides, poet and philosopher, was tempered by the Greek innate belief in *meden agan,* a principle of moderation in all things—the golden mean.

Fourth Day

Early on the morning of the fourth day the stadium once more was filled with spectators, eager to watch the final running of foot races. All morning long, the champions of the second day competed with each other for high honors. Sprinters and long-distance racers pounded down the raceway, urged on by cheers from a wildly enthusiastic crowd of more than 20,000. Winners of these events could now wear two olive crowns and carry in their hands the palm leaf awarded to double-winners.

After a simple lunch, crowds gathered in front of the Temple of Zeus for more boxing and wrestling among favorite athletes, each of whom was a champion. Then came the exhibition of the *pankration,* the free-for-all combination of wrestling and boxing. In the early days of this event, it was merely an exhibition, and by watching it the spectators gave vent to their inborn reaction to brutal battle; in the late fifth century B.C. the *pankration* was admitted to competition for which olive crowns were awarded.

In late afternoon of the fourth day, the crowds went back to the sloping banks of the stadium to watch the exhibition of armor racing. Clad only in helmet and shield, the armored racers, weighed down with bronze, sped down the stadium. After looking at hundreds of vase paintings of armor racing we suspect that these specialists could be quick-tempered if they lost. The one painting we see here shows the man who came in second throwing his shield to the ground, obviously in disgust and anger.

British Museum

Completion of armor race. Winner in center takes off his helmet and looks back in satisfaction as he sees the loser throw his shield to ground in disgust.

Perhaps we do these men a disservice by making this interpretation of the painting. But, the action occurs many times and, since much of our information comes from such illustrations, we cannot be too severely criticized for making a personal observation on the less-than-gentle nature of armored racers. With the armor racing, the athletic events of the Olympic Games were ended.

Fifth Day

A fifth day was given over to rejoicing and celebration, to final visits among friends who would not see each other for four more years, and to impromptu competitions among athletes. *Epheboi* sought instruction from experienced competitors and victors. Challenges among losers and winners were offered and taken; athletes went to the stadium to race, box, wrestle, throw the discus or javelin for the sheer joy of using their bodies in competition.

As the sun set on the fifth and closing day of the Olympics another procession formed at the *Prytaneion,* and wound its way for a final sacrifice at the Altar of Zeus. After the sacrifice the entire list of Olympic winners was read. The list was long and perhaps the judges asked that spectators hold their cheers and applause until the whole list was read (as is done today when the people at a banquet head-table are introduced); we can be certain that friends and admirers applauded and cheered as each victor was introduced (just as friends disregard the toastmaster today and applaud as each person is introduced).

When the ceremony was over, and a lamb sacrificed, the Games were officially at an end.

But, throughout the night, the green, luscious Valley of

Olympia was alive with singing and dancing.

Camp sites were broken up at dawn on the sixth day. Embassies and athletes said their goodbyes as in groups they began the long trek home.

Gradually Olympia became a place for quiet reverie; stadium, temples, and buildings would not be filled again with people until the next Olympics, four full years hence.

HONORS FOR VICTORS

Today's Olympic victor and today's winners of the high
school 440-yard dash readily understand the thrill of personal accomplishment experienced by the Olympic victor of
the golden age of Greece. Present-day Olympic medals and
track-meet ribbons are comparable to the wild olive-wreath
crown; medal, ribbon, and crown are all symbols of achievement and honor.

For the victor at Olympia the conferring of various
honors actually began as the sound of cheering in the

stadium died away; the moment of glory when the winner stood erect before the judges to be crowned was only the first of many occasions honoring the Olympic victor. His triumph, the culmination of training and education, was symbolic of a way of life, of a philosophy explicit in the beautiful and the good. The triumphal procession around the stadium, with the victor high on strong shoulders, the frenzied cheers, and the flowers cast by the spectators were for both the victor and for Greek standards he represented.

Paeans of praise sung for him applied to all that was revered in Greece. He received "honors befitting a citizen of high esteem": that line from a Victory Ode by Simonides is a key to the Greeks' respect for the citizen. The individual, the citizen, was the epitome of all that was good and worthy, and each man bore his title "citizen" with dignity and honor.

The citizen who was an Olympic victor was the most honored of mortals. The only attainment greater than winning "the crown at Olympia" would have been to take a place with the gods on Olympus, as the story of Diagoras of Rhodes illustrates.

Diagoras was a famous athlete, six-time winner at the Olympic Games, and son and grandson of Olympic victors. He was an elderly man when his sons, Damagetos and Ausilaos, won four crowns at the Olympic Games of 448 B.C. With affection and pride and a sincere demonstration of filial devotion, the two victors placed their crowns on the head of their father, whom they carried on their shoulders around the stadium. The group passed a friend who called out, "You had better die, Diagoras. You cannot get more. You cannot climb the summit to Mount

Olympus, can you?" No mortal could go to Olympus but the friend implied that only a place in the hall of the gods would bring greater honor to Diagoras. By inheritance, through the prowess of his own youth, and with the four wins by his two victor-sons, Diagoras approached immortality, the status of the gods on Olympus.

The proud father entertained five thousand guests at the victory banquet for his sons, and, when it was over, went to bed, sinking into a sleep from which he did not waken. He died in the night following the happy triumph. The next day at Olympia there was jubilant celebrating and rejoicing for Diagoras, the man who could die such a beautiful death. His sons bore his body back to their home island, Rhodes. Sons and grandsons inherited the character, the beauty of mind and body of Diagoras, until men of the family, known as the Diagoridae, had won forty-nine more Olympic crowns.

News of an Olympic victory was carried by fast runners or by charioteers to the victor's home city, where preparations for his return were begun at once. The celebration began with the triumphal entry of the victor into the city, with a procession greater in importance than that of a Roman Emperor because the Olympic victor was an individual honored for human values. The winner had achieved a symbolic victory, and adulation was given to him by his peers, free men of Greece, citizens all.

When a victor and his official Embassy neared the city, a runner carried the news of the approaching procession, and townspeople rushed out into the countryside to meet the victor, to shower him with flowers, and to sing his praises. A section of the town wall, which encompassed most Greek communities, was broken away for free access; it was thought that "no gate was good enough for the fair-limbed youth." Through the wide opening, the victor strode with measured step, his *himation* billowing about him. He proceeded at once to the city's chief temple to give thanks to his god or goddess for victory, and to pledge that so long as he lived, the victor would try to be worthy of the honor bestowed on him. All victors were aware that their honor carried with it weighty responsibility.

The olive crown was a constant reminder that much was expected of its recipient. He was a symbol of the highest moral values of the time in which he lived, and it was incumbent on him to speak and act in the finest traditions of *aidos*.

Youngsters sought his counsel on personal problems. *Epheboi*, trying to perfect their bodies at the gymnasium, asked his advice during practice sessions. Parents and teachers cited him as example to their children and pupils, and urged them on to the attainment of "supreme beauty of body, mind, and soul" achieved by the victor. Every action of his lifetime was expected to embody the highest moral standards. Achievement was not quickly forgotten as is sometimes the unfortunate case with today's heroes. Subsequent victors did not overshadow the Olympic winner; they took their places of honor with him.

The first joyous reception of the victor in procession and his visit to the temple were followed by feasts and banquets. As honored citizen, he sat with dignitaries on the front row of the city's amphitheater where performances of drama, dance, and music were presented.

Slowly the city returned to a pace of normal living, and

then, about two months after the victory, other celebrations were scheduled. One date was determined by the completion of a statue of the victor. The greatest sculptor available began working immediately after the victory at Olympia, producing either a statue carved in marble or one cast in bronze. With pomp and ceremony, the statue of the victor was erected in a prominent location; offerings were made to Zeus and to the local patron god or goddess. If the victor's family or his home city could afford a second statue, it was sent to Olympia for erection in the *Altis*. Every victor was given the privilege of having his victory perpetuated by such visual evidence at the scene of his triumph. Pausanias, the traveler and historian to whom we are so indebted for facts about the Olympic Games, reported that at one time in Olympia there were three thousand statues, each with an inscription commemorating a winner of the wild olive-wreath crown.

Erecting a statue in the victor's home city was a sacred duty, not something dependent on available funds. There is a story about one city that not only gave a halfhearted reception to its victor but also failed to erect a statue in his image. For eleven Olympics thereafter no athlete from the city was able to win a crown though many competitors were sent to Olympia. Finally officials of another generation vowed to the gods that, should an athlete from the city win, atonement would be made for the disgraceful action of the past. And, at the very next Olympic Games, the city did have a victor, to whom it erected a statue of gold and ivory.

A second honor, delayed like the ceremony of placing the statue, depended on the completion of a victory ode, an

Epinikia, written by a well-known poet, commissioned by the victor's family. In Greece there were many authors of *Epinikia;* these included Simonides, Bacchylides, and, the most famous of all, Pindar. Many of Pindar's victory odes

Statue in honor of an Olympic victor, showing youth binding a fillet, the ribbon of victory, around his head. Known as the Diadoumenos, this famous statue is typical of those placed in home towns of Olympic champions.

National Museum, Athens

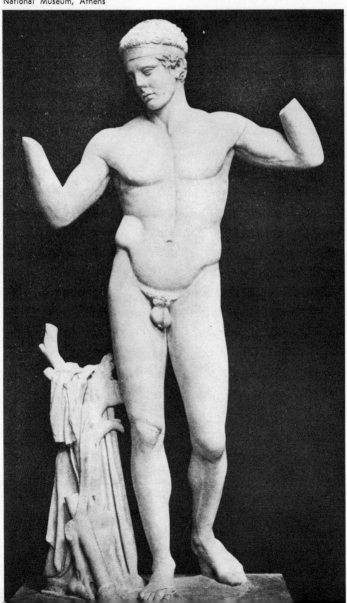

have been preserved and a reading of those lyrics brings a thrill of understanding of the high place held by an Olympic winner during the age of the poet. Between the lines of the storytelling odes, highlighted by panegyrics for the victor, one senses the ever-present tenets of *aidos* and *kalòs k'agathós*.

Pindar, member of an aristocratic family of Thebes, was born in 518 B.C., and lived to be an old man; the date of his death probably was 445 B.C., because his last known ode is dated 446 B.C. A professional poet of great reputation, he traveled through the Greek world, staying as guest of those for whom he wrote poems.

If a family could afford to pay Pindar's fee for an *Epinikia,* the poet began his writing by drawing on his knowledge of the performance of the victor. Pindar regularly attended the festival of the Olympic Games, and his powers of observation were so keen that he singled out every detail of every victor's performance. It is said, by a contemporary, that Pindar's eye was as trained as a judge's; that the poet could watch twenty men race and later recount in detail the movements of each runner.

His ode contained, in addition to the actions of the athlete, family references based on studies of genealogy. He learned the genealogy of the victor's family, tracing it back to some god or demigod; the history was lyrically woven into the story of the victor's performance at the Games. Praise to the youth was worded with poetic sensitivity so that the completed *Epinikia* was a masterpiece of lyric poetry. One of the longer odes by Pindar is the Eighth Olympic Ode, a typical work, part of which we have freely translated:

Olympia, mother of gold-crowned games,
mother of verity, where prophets seek
the favor of Zeus, search to know his pleasure
by making offerings in sacred flames;
ask what hope he has for those
straining for the victor's crown
after wearying training performed;
Zeus' will is found through pious prayer.
O, Pisan grove with feathery trees
receive our festival hymn with flowers.
Glorious is the fame henceforth
of him on whom your favor falls.
Many roads there are to sweet success
if the gods will bless his mortal toil.

Timosthenes, fate has given you and
your brother to Zeus. He gave you victory
at Nemean games; then on Alcimedon's brow
he placed the wreath of champion
at Olympia, too.
Graceful and virile to see, matching action
to beauty he was victorious at wrestling,
thereby adding glory to his homeland, Aegina,
fair island where above all they honor
Themis, friend of Zeus the Hospitable.

In his opening lines Pindar set the scene in Olympia,
giving homage to the sanctuary where contestants asked
for the blessing of Zeus. The poet then extolled the virtues
of men willing to devote fair bodies and fine minds to the
exhausting preparation for athletic competition. Painting a

glowing word picture of rewards heaped on victors, he named the victor in whose honor the Eighth Olympic Ode was written—the boy, Alcimedon of Aegina, an island not far from Athens.

To add glory to the boy's family, Pindar mentions that the victor's brother, Timosthenes, also was an Olympic champion, and that Alcimedon was a winner at the Nemean Games. Describing Alcimedon as fair of form, great with honor, and strong in action, Pindar then names the event (wrestling) won, and points out how Olympian an honor that win was for Alcimedon's home island, Aegina.

The poet continues with praise for the island of Aegina, illustrating through historical reference how many of the gods favored its citizens for valor. Pindar stresses the fact that Aeginatans were of Dorian descent, and noted throughout the world for their hospitality. With subtlety, he pays tribute to Melesias, famed trainer, who prepared Alcimedon for the Games at Olympia; Melesias himself was a champion with many honors. Linking trainer and victor, Pindar states that Alcimedon was the thirtieth winner trained by Melesias. Rounding out the ode, the poet presents a flowing panegyric of fair men, living and dead, who contributed to establishing the reputation of Aegina, the glorious island.

A victory ode was presented in public performance arranged by city officials and the father of the winner. An artistic spectacle, featuring dancers, choral groups, musicians, and actors, was given in the community amphitheater, with the victor as honored guest. When the occasion was celebrated with an elaborate production, the victory ode usually was sung; at more modest performances, it was recited.

The Olympic victor was not only honored at home; wherever he traveled in Greece, he enjoyed the privilege of eating and lodging in a city's *Prytaneion,* as guest of the priests in charge of that sacred building.

Olympic victory resulted in many benefits but the great honor was a difficult one to keep untarnished. Edith Hamilton, author of *The Greek Way* and other literary works about Greece and the Greeks, and herself officially honored as the First Lady of Athens by the Greek government, translated for us a passage from Pindar that succinctly expresses the essence of Olympic victory: "Before the gates of excellence, the high gods have placed sweat. Long is the road thereto and rough and steep. But when the height is achieved then is there duty so hard in keeping."

Terme Museum, Rome

CREEPING PROFESSIONALISM

It is a temptation to end a history of the ancient Olympic Games at a high point, at the climax of centuries when true Greek character dominated the athletic events. But the chronicle would be at once incomplete and misleading, and total truth that includes the unfortunate deterioration of the Games is essential if we are to keep the ideal of *aidos* which dominated the ages of glory. There were centuries marked by the decline which seems to strike every civilization, when personal dignity, uncommon deeds, and individual responsibility give way to the stultifying dominance of unworthy men.

Regrettably, the philosophy of sport-for-sport's-sake waned in Greece. With changing times and passing centuries, lavish prizes were presented to winners of athletic contests. Young men began to compete for treasure, for lifetime subsidy, and negotiable prizes; gone was the joy of competition and of pride in the honor of victory.

The increase of gold-rich rewards to athletes coincided with the decline of Greek culture and democracy, with the decay of the very nation. Greece, torn by inner strife, by civil war, became lax in character and morals. The way was open for foreign invasion, occupation, and rule. In a gradually developed welfare state, every citizen expected the government to take care of him. Slowly Greeks became members of a socialized state; no longer were they part of a proud nation in which each individual expressed personal dignity and accepted responsibility for himself and for his country.

Degeneration was accompanied by the rise of professionalism in athletics. Mobs gathered to watch hired professionals who were cosseted and coddled by promoters of cities eager to have winners at the four athletic festivals of Greece. The situation was not unlike one that exists today in certain sports to which undergraduate athletes are attracted by scholarships and fringe benefits offered by educational institutions that expect to have winning teams on the football field and the basketball court. Subsidy and professionalism threaten amateur sportsmanship in any age.

In the seventh, sixth, and fifth centuries B.C., Greek athletes had bodies co-ordinated from head to toe, and were trained to participate with skill and enthusiasm in several sports. Like other Greeks, the athletes subsisted on a diet of vegetables and fish, consuming very little meat.

By the beginning of the fourth century, professional athletes, proficient at one sport only, were firmly entrenched. Disregard for principles of the past resulted in the era of hired professionals. Cities recruited farm boys, young miners and sheepherders, all chosen for strength and stamina. They were trained for one event, with concentration on specific parts of the body, not on a well-proportioned physique. The athlete was encouraged in specialized body-building by irresponsible officials and citizens interested only in a winner, whatever the cost in cash or to sportsmanship.

Professional runners, who performed exercises that gave them vast lung power and powerful legs, wasted no time on the development of their arms and shoulders. Discus throwers, developing arms and shoulders massive enough to hurl the discus with precision and strength, but without grace, walked about on spindly legs, underdeveloped and weak. Wrestlers had unattractively muscled arms, chests, and bull-like necks; boxers had grotesquely corded muscles bulging from shoulders and arms.

Professionals were listless and dull-witted, muscle-bound and clumsy except in the event for which they were specifically trained. They spent their days working on muscles while compatriots stood around admiring the display of brute strength. In the late fifth and early fourth centuries special trainers devised routines of exercise and diets for athletic bruisers. Their gargantuan appetites were satisfied with vast quantities of meats that provided protein for muscular bulk. Sokrates is said to have commented vividly on how revolted he was at "the sight of these beasts in human form snarling while they gorged on raw meat."

Herodikas of Selymbria and Pythagoras of Samos were two of the famous trainers of professionals; these two men and others experienced in training by special techniques forced the professionals to do their bidding. The trainers handled their doltish charges with driving insensitivity. Cities hired trainers to scout for potential athletes who were made citizens and, and as such represented the community at athletic festivals.

The depraved condition of athletes and officials controlling festivals was not total even as late as the beginning of the third century B.C. A few amateurs clung to the glory of the past, reflecting the shining example; according to Pausanias, amateurs "kept alive the old traditions of fine-limbed contestants." Records of the four festivals of Greece are highlighted with exciting contests between the amateurs and the professionals, contests in which the adherents to tradition were often victorious.

Decrease in moral standards and athletic ideals, and increase in paid professional performances inevitably resulted in a creeping corruption. Records of the Nemean, Pythian, and Isthmian Games indicate that more and more bribes were offered and taken both by contestants and judges. Philip of Macedon, after his usurpation of Greek rule, defied the judges at Olympia and had himself crowned supreme victor at the Games. There is historical evidence of other corruption at Olympia, the last stronghold of true sportsmanship.

At the 96th Olympics, in 396 B.C., two bribed judges insisted on awarding the olive crown for the *stade* race to Eupolimus of Elis; a third judge, honest and incorruptible, doggedly held to his unprejudiced decision, and awarded the honor of victor to Leon of Ambakia. Leon publicly accused the two judges of bribery, appealed to the high council, and won his case and his wild olive-wreath crown. That disgrace was one of the first examples of bribery at Olympia and even those willing to hire paid professionals were shocked: they condoned similar action at the other festivals but not at Olympia, Sanctuary of Zeus!

Eupolus, son of Dionysius of Thessaly, bribed his opponents in boxing to let him win at the 98th Olympic Games, in 388 B.C. The collusion was discovered, and fines of the conspirators produced a sum of money large enough for five bronze statues of Zeus in the *Altis*. The statues, called *zanes,* were set up at the tunneled entrance to the stadium as warnings to all athletes. For his act of bribery, Eupolus was banished from Thessaly along with his father and their family.

Sotades of Crete was approached with a bribe from the officials of Ephesus just before the opening of the 99th Olympic Games in 384 B.C. The young Cretan seemed to be almost certain of victory in wrestling and the *pentathlon*, events for which the town of Ephesus had no possible winner. Accepting terms and the offer of rich rewards, Sotades renounced his Cretan citizenship and, contending as a citizen of Ephesus, did become a victor. When officials refused to list the victory, Sotades was of no further use to the Ephesians, who disclaimed him. For his disloyalty to Crete, Sotades was banished from his home island and, as a man without citizenship, wandered from place to place for the rest of his life.

Some stories tell of offered bribes being haughtily refused, of honor triumphant. When Antipater, son of Kleon of Miletus, was favored to win the boys' boxing event at Olympia, Dionysius, Tyrant of Syracuse, sent a messenger to ask Kleon to allow his son to become a citizen of Syracuse. Accepting a large sum of money, Kleon agreed, and gave the order to Antipater, who sulked, though he had no choice in the matter.

As predicted, Antipater was winner of the boxing matches, and Kleon, Dionysius, and other Syracusans were overjoyed, but only briefly. Antipater walked across the stadium and stood for a minute, looking his father in the eyes; then the youth turned and moved on to the judges' stand. As the chief judge stood, crown in hand, Antipater called for silence and exposed the conspiracy between his father and Dionysius. A hush fell as Antipater explained why he was unworthy to wear the crown. The judges consulted and then, to wild cheers, placed the crown on Antipater's head, commending him for his feat and *aidos*. Kleon was banished from his home city of Miletus; the Syracusan Embassy, headed by the hated tyrant, was forced to leave Olympia in disgrace.

Most officials and judges tried to keep the name Olympia free from scandal, and to retain the place as a center for traditional athletic events. Those Greeks closed ranks to protect the sanctity and character of that one festival.

Alexander the Great, aware that the pre-eminence of Olympic Games was a cohesive factor in Greek culture, did all he could to preserve their high standards. The wily and canny conqueror of the Greeks endeavored to restore Olympic prestige, to regulate professionalism and thereby curtail corruption. His power was so great that, even under several of his successors, Olympia returned to the high ideals of athletic competition—for a time.

Professionalism completely infiltrated Olympia during the second and first centuries B.C., and decadence was complete in the first three centuries A.D. Roman conquests whittled away crumbling remains of stalwart character; brutish Roman athletes and even depraved Roman rulers competed in games at Olympia.

In spite of the miserable state of the Olympic Games, the Valley of Olympia, and the events held in it, created an aura that could not be completely extinguished. Any man who made a pilgrimage to the valley still was recognized as a person of esteem in his home community where he was pointed out as "one who went to Olympia."

Games were debauched and braggarts with brute strength stomped through the *Altis* every four years. But even the most insensitive had some feeling about the mysterious power of Olympia and abided by the ban on women. Romans, who traveled with their concubines through Greece, left the ladies of pleasure at encampments outside the limits of the Valley of Olympia.

The end of the Games was ordered in A.D. 393 by Emperor Theodosius, a Christian who branded them as mere pagan rites. Thus ended, in ignominy, games first recorded in 776 B.C.; games which flourished for 1,169 years of recorded history, and for untold previous years, not recorded or reported by historians.

By the fourth century A.D., many statues and treasured

objects of the *Altis* had been carried away to Rome; the chryselephantine statue of Zeus melted down for its gold. The *Altis* was almost stripped bare, with only a few treasures overlooked by plunderers, probably quite by chance.

Theodosius, a diabolical and vicious tyrant, ordered the temples toppled and the few remaining statues destroyed. In spite of the destruction, a few buildings stood until Olympia was laid in ruins by an earthquake in A.D. 521. After that, the Kladeos River changed its course, covering much of the sanctuary with silt and mud. Wind and rain weathered the site, which was completely entombed by later earthquakes.

The dark shadow, that so insidiously spread with athletic professionalism and darkened with bribery, finally eclipsed what had been one of the glories of Greece. Olympia and its games were obliterated and forgotten.

Centuries passed, and scholars reading Pausanias, Pindar, and other authors were impressed by the ancient history of Olympia. Some learned men traveled to Olympia, riding in donkey carts over dusty miles before descending into the verdant valley where evergreens and wild olive trees grew over the hard earth. In the mid-eighteenth century Richard Chandler, a British archaeologist, did more than travel to Olympia, to look and dream. He dug. Before he had to stop for lack of funds, he had uncovered some ancient walls.

In 1852, Ernst Curtius, an energetic young German, determined and idealistic, decided that he wanted "Olympia exhumed and brought to life." Curtius, who received funds for excavation from the King of Germany, promised the

Greek government to work under the direction of an official agency and to leave any finds from Olympia in Greece.

Curtius and other archaeologists gave Olympia back to the world. Dirt and debris were cleared away and, in time, the *Bouleuterion, Prytaneion, palaestra,* and part of the gymnasium were uncovered, their foundations and floors laid bare. Foundations of temples and treasuries were exposed. Massive six-foot-in-diameter drums of ancient columns were dug up, cleaned, and piled on top of each other to reconstruct the pillars which had stood around ancient temples.

The magnificent statue of Hermes done by Praxiteles, fourth century B.C. sculptor, was recovered from rubble; in all the warmth of its flesh-toned marble it is now a prized exhibit at the Olympia Museum. The "Winged Victory" by the sculptor Paionius once stood high on a pedestal at the east end of the Temple of Zeus; today, restored by experts, it can be seen floating high toward the ceiling of the Olympia Museum. Also in the Museum there are *halteres,* shields, *strygils,* and records inscribed on stone; and many of the thousands of bronze statuettes dug up by official excavators. Marble statues that stood in the east and west pediments of the Temple of Zeus are displayed at the Museum, the figures battered but beautiful.

German archaeologists excavating at Olympia discovered the site of the workshop of Pheidias, the famed sculptor of the fifth century B.C., who designed and constructed the forty-foot-high statue of the seated Zeus for the temple bearing that god's name. While working at the workshop site in 1959, archaeologists found a clay cup which had on its bottom the inscription that translated means "I belong to Pheidias." The very cup from which Pheidias drank!

REBIRTH OF THE OLYMPICS

Olympia—the valley, the sanctuary, and the games—slept for fifteen centuries. Brutal displays of blood and gore in Roman arenas took the place of the noble contests of the Greeks. Jousting and hunting were sporting highlights of the Middle Ages. Other contests, other games, for centuries, dimmed the glory that was Olympia's.

Olympia, fable, myth, fantasy from the past, began to intrigue men after the discovery and translation of the poems of Pindar, the history of Herodotus, the travel books of Pausanias. Olympia lived again in the minds of men inspired by poetry and prose penned by ancient writers.

In the middle of the nineteenth century, a young French-man was stirred by the epic grandeur of the Olympic idea; at the same time, he was deeply concerned about the state of his world in which country was armed against country. Could Olympic Games, in revival, unite the world as they had in ancient times? In the fervent hope that such a great thing might happen, he traveled throughout Europe, Great Britain, and the United States in an effort to make his dream of peace come true.

That Frenchman was a wealthy, titled Parisian, Baron Pierre de Coubertin, who had the money and time to pursue an ideal. Gradually the Baron sparked intense interest in a revival of the quadrennial games; or quinquennial games, as you choose. Reference to either a four-year or five-year period between Olympic Games, ancient and modern, causes some written confusion and often leads to errors of fact about the ancient games. A full four years elapses between the Olympic Games; in a sense they are quadrennial. But Olympics are held in the fifth year following; in that sense they are quinquennial. For example, the Olympic Games were held in Rome, Italy, in 1960; at the close of the Olympics at Rome, the count of calendar years until the next Olympics was made: 1961, 1962, 1963, 1964, an elapsed time of four full years; but the Olympic Games at Tokyo, Japan, were scheduled for 1964, the fifth year after 1960.

The ancient Greeks figured the date of their games by the passage of four full years from the previous celebration of the festival; that put the date in the fifth year. In the stadium at Delphi, there is a stone altar on which is carved five rings symbolic of the quinquennial timing for the celebrated games. The design of five circles on the Delphi altar is today the symbol of the Olympic Games; the circles form a link between ancient and modern Olympics.

Altar in stadium at Delphi, with the five rings indicating the quidquennial spacing of the games. These five rings were adopted by modern Olympics as their official symbol.

Samivel Photo

Convincing modern nations to revive the Olympic Games was a task to which Baron de Coubertin was dedicated. He first received the enthusiastic support of a few influential friends, and then he slowly infected others with the Olympic spirit. He addressed students and educators at universities, colleges, and high schools; lectured to groups of industrial leaders and philanthropists, to all who would listen.

Representatives of one nation and then another and another agreed to send athletes to Greece for competition in the first modern Olympic Games. Athens was chosen as the city for the Olympic contests because Olympia was remote and difficult to reach by donkey cart over dusty, rutty roads, some only primitive trails.

Baron de Coubertin, delighted by his success in promoting an Olympics revival, came to a point at which it seemed that the plan might fall through. It was necessary to build a costly marble stadium at Athens for the events; the site selected was one that had been occupied by a stadium in the sixth century B.C. Though wealthy, the Baron was not rich enough to build the stadium with his own funds; money poured in from many countries and many sources but the total was far short of the amount needed. When the situation seemed all but hopeless to the Baron, help came from George Averoff, a prominent Greek, who subscribed one million drachma to the stadium fund. Construction began. King George I of Greece agreed to be the official host for the Olympics. Athletes all over the world practiced for the Games while Athens prepared to receive them.

The date set for the first modern Olympic Games was

April, 1896.

Teams of athletes were pledged by Denmark, England, France, Germany, Hungary, Switzerland, the United States and, of course, Greece. The United States team was sponsored by the Boston Athletic Association and supported by funds raised through the efforts of the Honorable Oliver Arms, philanthropist and former Governor of Massachusetts. The American team included:

Arthur Blake ..... long-distance runner
Thomas Burke ..... sprinter
E. H. Clark ..... all-round athlete, best known as a broad jumper
Thomas Curtis ..... runner and hurdle jumper
William Hoyt ..... pole vaulter
John Paine
Sumner Paine ..... } brothers who were pistol-shot experts

This group was augmented, fortunately, by James B. Connolly and Robert L. Garrett. Young Connolly, a jumper, excited by the Olympics, applied to the administration of Harvard University, where he was a student, for permission to join the American team. The decision to refuse his request cheated Harvard of an honor that it never can claim. Student Connolly would not abide by the ruling and left school, for which action he was expelled by Harvard.

Princeton student, Robert Garrett, had better luck with the university where he was captain of the track team; his own sport was the shot-put. When he received permission to be away from Princeton, he asked the American team if he might join them, and was enthusiastically accepted. Robert Garrett had been fascinated by what he read about the discus throw, and, with the help of the Professor of Classics at Princeton, learned everything possible about the ancient sport. After long practice of the early style of throwing, he sailed for Greece.

Athletes from foreign countries were cordially received by the Greeks, who well deserve their reputation for hospitality and enthusiasm. Guest athletes were housed, and wined and dined, and provided with adequate practice fields. Then, as in ancient times, visitors from many lands began to gather for the history-making games. Reporters converged on Athens.

The dream of Baron de Coubertin was about to become reality. Olympic Games, suspended since A.D. 393, were to be held on Greek soil.

The morning of April 6, 1896, dawned with the brilliance for which Greece is known. Clear skies over Athens reflected the deep blue of the Aegean waters, just a few miles away. Iridescent dust from the hills made the air shimmer and gleam. Warm air was cooled by breezes blowing in from the sea. Crowds jammed the streets leading to the pure-white marble stadium which quickly filled with throngs of spectators. Those on the top rows were able to view the splendors of Athens and its environs. To the left was an impressive ancient building, the Temple of Olympian Zeus; and beyond it the Parthenon standing timelessly, majestically on the Akropolis. To the right, deep-colored evergreen trees covered the steep slopes of Mount Lykabettos. Spreading across the distant horizon were the fabled honey hills of Hymettos. The magnificent past and exciting present merged.

At 10:00 A.M. spines tingled at the sound of a flourish

of trumpets and the ruffle of drums. The thousands of spectators rose with a mighty cheer that might have produced echoes from the stadium at faraway Olympia. King George I of Greece, leading the procession into the stadium, was followed by members of the royal family and his ministers of the Cabinet. Behind the King and his retinue were members of the Greek diplomatic corps, and foreign Ambassadors and Consuls. The athletes came last, each group displaying the flag of its country; the contestants moved as nobly as the competitors who, at Olympia centuries earlier, passed through the tunnel into the stadium for the ancient Olympic Games.

King George welcomed official representatives of foreign countries, visitors from near and far, and the athletes; these then took an oath to contend with honor and fair play. A sacred flame, brought from a fire kindled in the ancient *Prytaneion* at Olympia, lighted an altar fire in the Athens stadium. The first modern Olympic Games had begun!

The first competition was a jumping event, called the "hop, step, jump." The contestants stood behind a line like the ancient *balbis,* and from it took a hop, one broad step, and then crouched for the spring into a broad jump. Sportswriters reported the tension in the air, an emotional electricity that seemed to flick like sparks from one spectator to another. Perhaps the emotion was generated by the thrill of watching the first Olympic event since A.D. 393; perhaps, by the appreciation of the supple skill of the jumpers. Whatever the basis for the reaction, the official Greek chronicler wrote, "From the moment the first GO was given . . . throughout the crowd ran a ripple, a thrilling sense of destiny . . . we were among the favored few watching the rebirth of the very essence of all that is fine in Greek culture."

Silence spread over the stadium as a contestant walked to the *balbis* to compete: after he completed the hop, step, jump, he was cheered and applauded. Every performance was carefully watched by judges, as in the old days. But form and grace were not considered; only distance counted in modern judging. Criteria had changed.

The young American, James B. Connolly, the ex-student at Harvard, expelled for attending the games, was the winner of the jumping event. With great ceremony, he was accompanied to the judges' stand, where he stood erect as a wild olive-wreath crown cut from a tree at Olympia was placed on his head. He was the first man to feel the touch of the crown since A.D. 393 when the Olympics were banned by Theodosius. It is reported that the winner's first words, after receiving the crown, were, "All my life I shall be weighted with responsibility." Fifteen centuries had not changed the feeling of honor and responsibility experienced by an Olympic winner. It is unlikely that James Connolly had studied or knew about the responsibilities of the ancient winners; his reaction probably was instinctive. The spirit of the Olympics was so alive that he felt he must always measure up to the honor.

The discus throw was the second event of the 1896 Olympic Games. The contestants had decided that, for the first revival of the Games, it was fitting to hurl the discus in the ancient style, rather than in the modern manner. The athlete favored to win the event was a handsome, powerful young Greek, Georgius Paraskevopoulos. He was *kalòs k'agathós*, beautiful of body and mind, and seemed to be fashioned from the very molds used to cast bronze statues of winners of ancient Olympics. Because the discus throw is uniquely Greek, it would seem likely that Paraskevopoulos was crowned winner. He wasn't.

Robert Garrett, Princeton University student, whose home was in Baltimore, Maryland, was also *kalòs k'agathós* and remained so through his years as a civic and cultural leader in Baltimore where it was our privilege to know him. Powerful and lithe, the American athlete stepped to the *balbis* on April 6, 1896; he tossed the discus 95 feet, which was six feet, seven and one-half inches farther than his "fine-formed" Greek competitor. Garrett immediately was given an *abrazo,* a hug and a kiss, by Paraskevopoulos, who escorted the victor to the judges' stand to receive the crown, the second man to wear the wild olive wreath in modern times. Later, Robert Garrett won another crown, for heaving the shot-put.

Robert Garrett, the Princeton athlete who won the discus throw in the first modern Olympic games held in Athens, Greece, in 1896. Garrett used the ancient method of throwing the discus to win his olive crown.

Courtesy of Garrett Family

Event followed event as the Olympic Games continued. Revelry with songs in Athens rivaled the ancient feasts given around the fires on the hills above Olympia. Several men present at the first modern Olympics have told us that everyone was aware of the affinity between past and present. Without planning, the stream of life by day and night flowed in confluence with the spirit of the past. Since the 1896 Games, a number of scholars have written aesthetic papers about the unmistakable but intangible commingling of past with present during the first modern Olympics. The spirit had lived through the centuries; it had not changed.

The Olympics planning committee for the 1896 Games added new competitions, competitions unheard of in ancient times. One of these was the now-famous race, listed on the 1896 program as "evidence of the Greek dedication to freedom as a nation, and the sacrifice of the individual to maintain that freedom."

The race honored Pheidippides who ran from Marathon to Athens in 490 B.C. to announce the Athenian victory over the invading Persians; the distance was to be the same covered by Pheidippides. When time for the modern marathon event came, the air was tense in Athens. Not a single Greek had won at the Olympic Games. If the national pride was hurt, the Greek hosts gave no outward sign, but many Greeks must have wondered whether one of their countrymen would win the long-distance race from Marathon.

One of the least likely to win was a boy unknown to Athenians. He was Spiridon Louys from the hills, a boy who tended bleating sheep; sometimes following his flock, at other times, guiding it for miles through grazing country.

The shepherd boy's heart was as courageous as the wolves he had to kill. His legs were strong and his stamina was great. He was so swift in motion that he could catch the hares that he broiled over his lonely fire in the hills.

Spiridon heard about the marathon race from travelers passing through the hills. With typical Greek sensitivity to the glories of the past, Spiridon was fascinated by the news of the Olympic Games; his imagination was fired by the event that was to begin at nearby Marathon. Leaving his flock with a brother, Spiridon went down to the plains of Marathon from which the Greeks long before had driven the Persians out into the Aegean Sea. After he was accepted for the race, the young shepherd fasted and prayed for two days and two nights; religious fervor and national pride swelled in the modest youth.

At dawn on the day of the long-distance race, contestants gathered for the start. By coincidence there were 25 runners for the 25-mile race to the stadium at Athens. On signal the racers were off with the famous French runner, Jean Lemursiaux, in the lead. The runners sped through ravines, over mountains, up and down zigzag paths, and along flat dusty paths. As they passed through little villages, peasants handed them cups of retsina, the local resinated wine, and gave them chunks of strengthening dark bread. The pace was grueling over terrain that was rugged. One by one runners dropped out, admitting defeat.

Riders near Athens finally sent in word that Lemursiaux was in the lead and the Greek boy, Spiridon, trailed the field. Then suddenly the Greeks in the stadium at Athens dared to hope for victory. Lemursiaux and Spiridon, now only five miles away, *were running neck and neck!*

With three miles to go, the shepherd boy took the lead. Could he hold it? Would the experienced Lemursiaux withhold a last spurt of speed and power to be used as he came down the broad avenue leading to the stadium? Every athlete of every nation fervently hoped that Spiridon would not falter, that he would be the victor.

When the word came that Spiridon Louys was jogging toward the stadium, well in the lead, King George spoke earnestly to his sons, Prince Constantine and Prince George. The youthful princes vaulted from their seats and sprinted across the stadium to the entrance. There they met Spiridon. Flanked by the two Greek princes, both over six feet tall, the shepherd entered the stadium and raced across the finish line.

Not a man remained seated. The air was split with a continuous roar of deafening noise. Tears streamed down the faces of the weak, the strong, the young, the old; a surge of emotion swept through the crowd. An American reporter wrote of the scene, "We all wept without shame, so greatly did the scene affect us. Such solidarity among nations is unknown and could this moment be preserved there would never be another war. What a pity. The spell will be broken and it really needn't be, if economics of nations did not prevent continuance of understanding among human beings. Yet, with all, this is a day to be cherished."

Spiridon, the shepherd boy from the hills, was crowned with the wild olive wreath, the first Greek to be so honored in modern times. Reporters wrote glowingly about the modesty of Spiridon, who accepted the honor with grave dignity, and the courtly manner which is typically Greek. The victor seemed confused when valuable gifts were presented to him, and by offers from excited compatriots: A tailor in Athens offered to make his clothes free of charge for as long as the tailor lived. A fisherman wanted to send fresh fish each day to the boy's home in the hills. A barber said he would serve the boy weekly, if he could get to Athens. A *taverna* owner offered free meals to Spiridon for life.

No one knows what happened to Spiridon Louys, after he quietly returned to his hills and his sheep, taking with him the joyous memory of his triumph for Greece, his native land.

So great was the success of the first modern Olympics Games that an international committee was established to plan for succeeding Games. The Olympics were at Paris, France, in 1900; in the United States at St. Louis, Missouri, in 1904; again in Athens in 1906; in London in 1908, and at Stockholm, Sweden, in 1912. Those ended in good fellowship with athletes and officials planning to meet again in 1916. Their plans were shattered.

World War I began and, unlike the Greeks of ancient times, modern men did not declare an Olympic Truce in order to hold the Games. Games also were suspended during World War II.

Today we have the most sophisticated technology ever known to man. Perhaps in the future our sense of moral values will catch up with our materialistic progress.

Every four years, unless there is a war, an impressive ceremony is held by this modern marble altar on a slope overlooking the ancient sanctuary of Olympia. A sacred fire is lighted; a runner dips his torch into its flames, and races across the Kladeos River, up a hill, down through the modest, modern town of Olympia, and jogs his way along the road leading up and out of the soft green valley. A few kilometers ahead, he meets a waiting runner who takes the torch to another relay point. The torch passes from runner to runner until the last one reaches a Greek port where the torch is placed aboard a ship and carried across the sea. From a distant port, the torch is taken by relay runners to the place where the modern Olympics is being held. At ceremony time, a final runner enters the stadium, races down the concourse to the Olympic altar where flame from the torch lights a fire that burns throughout the Olympic Games.

The flame of Olympia that still burns from Greece to wherever the Games are held links the ancient past with the present.

Marble altar at Olympia where the Olympic flame is lighted and carried to the site of each modern Game.

HIGH DESTINY

Modern Olympic meets are lineal descendants of the most famous of ancient games that were quadrennially the focal point of the entire Greek world. And modern Olympic gatherings are by no means the sole inheritors of the ancient *Olympic spirit.*

Numerous contemporary athletic associations and even a few educational institutions maintain the spirit of athletic events held in individual Greek communities. One such modern organization is the Turnverein, founded at Berlin, in 1811, by Frederick Ludwig Jahn; he established centers where the youth of Germany could meet and build a way of life stressing mental, physical, patriotic and spiritual values. Participating in all sports for sheer joy, Turnverein members spread throughout the world; they became proficient in gymnastics, in field and track events, in boxing, wrestling and discus throwing. Many Turnverein athletes were chosen to compete in modern Olympic contests. Turnvereiners continue to enjoy sport-for-sport's sake.

A similar movement for developing the whole human being is the *Sokol,* meaning falcon, the swift daring bird which is the symbol of the association composed chiefly of people of Czechoslovakian descent. The first Sokol unit was founded at Prague, in 1862, by Miroslav Tyrs; the unit's tenets were based on Dr. Tyrs' intimate knowledge of the ancient Greeks' passionate desire to achieve the peak of well-rounded human performance. By 1940 there were more than a million Sokol members in Czechoslovakia; each man dedicated to physical, mental, religious and cultural development. The first American Sokol was established at St. Louis, in 1865; today more than a quarter of a million Sokol members in the United States range in age from six to sixty, and each strives for personal perfection.

Body-building and weight-lifting, on a rise of popularity after World War II, attracted numerous exhibitionists who, developing tremendous biceps, preened themselves with mirrored-pleasure and admired every new rope-like muscle. Gradually the narcissism of the fad gave way to body-building by young men and women intent on creating the sound bodies befitting human beings with fine minds. Richard Manson, posed in the photograph heading this chapter, is an example of a body builder who has a wide intellectual background. As a high school student he was a debater, participant in dramatics as well as all-round athlete. He was president of the Baltimore Junior Natural History

Club, a member of the Young Scientists Club and the Maryland Ornithological Society. At the University of Maryland he majored in economics before taking a master of arts degree in political science. Today he holds a responsible business position, and continues his interest in athletics, theater and natural history.

Today a rapidly-increasing number of young and middle-aged people are forming clubs for physical conditioning, a state of being no longer scorned. Groups like the Turnverein and Sokol, based on national inheritance, are active everywhere. In Scandinavian countries, effervescent people, working toward physical fitness, are spurred on by the sense of vitality and joy achieved through co-ordinated exercises. There are nearly 300 athletic clubs in Stockholm alone.

Each of the hundreds of modern groups, distributed worldwide, contributes its share of Olympic winners; in America, no association produces more victors than the Junior Olympics. The Junior Olympic program of the United States Amateur Athletic Union is a competitive recreation program designed to develop a spirit of true sportsmanship and fair play, as well as the physical, mental and moral improvement of the youth of the nation. In 1949, the United States Olympic Association, prompted to action by innumerable abuses in the use of the word *Olympic,* delegated the AAU as the official organization to administer the Junior Olympic program.

Inaugurated originally as a track and field program for boys and girls between the ages of six and sixteen, the expanded program includes swimming, diving, gymnastics and wrestling. More than a million youngsters now participate in those sports in hundreds of communities; each community registers its Junior Olympic winners with the parent organization. The U.S. Olympic Association hopes to develop the program into an international Junior Olympics to be held every four years in conjunction with the senior Olympics. The plan is not yet a reality, but one day juniors, like those of ancient Greece, will have their own Olympic meets at which the youth of many nations will compete.

The American Junior Olympic program already has resulted in high achievement. Records show that 38% of the Americans competing in the last three Olympics were once participants in a local Junior Olympic program. With one exception, all members of the 1960 U.S. Olympic Swimming Teams, men and women, came up through the ranks of the AAU Junior Olympic program. Rafer Johnson, one of many outstanding American track and field stars in 1960 competition at the Rome Olympics, first attracted notice as a young athlete in Junior Olympic events. Thousands of Junior Olympic athletes have gone to colleges and universities where they have achieved academic records commensurate with their physical capabilities.

More and more academic institutions are stressing sport-for-sport's sake instead of sports for financial gain. As long ago as 1934, The Johns Hopkins University activated a revolutionary program that did away with gate receipts for athletic contests; the public was invited to attend Hopkins athletics events free of charge. The athletic program, like every academic department, is supported by funds included in the University's budget. Hopkins receives no portion of gate receipts from games or events when its athletes play or compete at other universities or colleges; visiting teams, playing at Hopkins, receive no remuneration. In its own league, Hopkins consistently wins at various competitions and sports; outside its league, it has long been famous for the top-quality of its lacrosse team. Hopkins lacrosse teams represented the United States at the Olympic games of 1928 in Amsterdam and 1932 in Los Angeles.

The same type of athletic program has been adopted by the University of the South at Sewanee, Tennessee. The University, better known as Sewanee, is well-known for academic excellence, and for experimenting with new areas of study. In 1962, without fanfare, Sewanee inaugurated an exciting program in Greek athletics that is a cooperative effort of the Department of Classical Languages and the Physical Education Department. The course, Classics-206, is typical of Sewanee's emphasis on Classical studies, which may account for the high percentage of Rhodes and Fulbright scholars from the University of the South.

Classics-206 is designed to teach, through practice, the Greek concept of athletics in relationship to total education; and, by comparison, the influence of ancient sports on the modern. Students, learning how the spirit of *aidos* can be incorporated into 20th-century life, are instructed in the ancient techniques of boxing, wrestling, running, the discus throw, the shot-put, and javelin hurling.

The idea for Classics-206 was born one spring day by faculty members enjoying a coffee break. Two Classics professors, Bayly Turlington and Charles M. Binniker, Jr., discussing athletic source material, fired the enthusiasm of Ted Bitondo, Sewanee's Director of Physical Education. The three men developed a plan for a "laboratory" to supplement classroom lectures.

Registration for the trial run of the course totaled

twelve; a Classics major, four other students taking some work in the Classics department, and seven athletes attracted by the novel idea. Professors Turlington and Binniker, alternate lecturers for the weekly class, presented the philosophy of Greek athletics and the place of athletics in Greek life. Lantern slides illustrated the various sports of Greece as depicted on vase paintings and in sculpture. Reading assignments of original source material, including Pindar's *Odes* to victorious athletes, acquainted the students with the essence of Greek athleticism.

Once a week, Classics-206 met in the athletic laboratory with Coach Bitondo as the *paidotribe*, the trainer for youth-

Coach Bitondo shows Classics-206 student the correct manner of throwing the discus, Greek style.

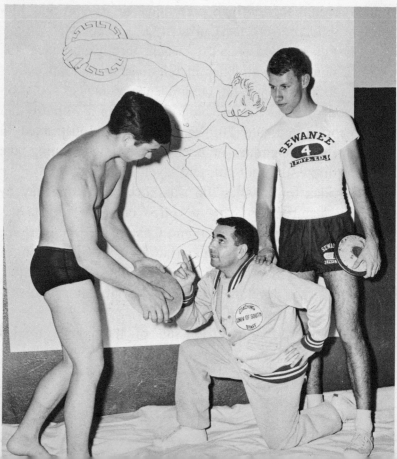

ful Sewanee *Hellenes*. The student-contestant used hand-wraps, instead of leather thongs, for Greek-style boxing, and learned both ancient and modern techniques for all track and field sports. Shot and discus were carved of rock dug from an off-campus quarry.

Sewanee physically is situated not far from Athens, Georgia; in spirit, it is closer to Athens, Greece, thousands of geographical miles away.

Reports of Sewanee's Classics-206, successful in its first season, spread through a grapevine to amateur athletes in schools and clubs. Inquiries poured into Sewanee from those eager to establish a similar athletic program con-

Hurling the javelin in modern style, this Sewanee student has previously practiced with a Greek-style javelin propelled by a leather thong.

sistent with the ancient Greek belief that a fine mind in a fair form would produce a nation of superior human beings.

The relatively small population of ancient Greece created a culture so profound that its impact still influences the lives of men today. Greeks achieved their pre-eminence through the concept that the greatest creation on earth is the soul of man, and that it is basic to man to combine the highest order of mind, spirit, and body. The unique philosophy gave birth to the idea of freedom of the individual, to the theory that man is answerable only to himself, and not to some tyrant determined to own, body and soul, those under his rule.

The ideal in athletics was one vital segment of the total contribution of ancient Greece to which we are heirs. We owe a debt for the emergence of democracy, for written laws, for developments in art and architecture, in philosophy and literature.

Twenty-four hundred years ago, the Greek historian, Thucydides, wrote, "The kind of events that once took place will by reason of human nature take place again." The contemporary resurgence of amateur athletics and widespread physical education programs, combined with intellectual and spiritual training, may lead modern man to the ultimate in human perfection typified by the ancient Greeks at the height of their civilization.

Through the centuries there has been no change in the truth of Plato's words: "There can be no fairer spectacle than that of a man who combines the possession of moral goodness in his soul, with the outward beauty of his body; corresponding and harmonizing with the former because the same great pattern enters into both if a man is eventually to achieve his high destiny."

DATES OF MODERN OLYMPIC GAMES

	YEAR	PLACE	WINNER
1st	1896	Athens	U.S.A.
2nd	1900	Paris	U.S.A.
3rd	1904	St. Louis	U.S.A.
4th	1906	Athens	U.S.A.
5th	1908	London	U.S.A.
6th	1912	Stockholm	U.S.A.
	1916	None — W.W.I.	
7th	1920	Antwerp	U.S.A.
8th	1924	Paris	U.S.A.
		(First Winter Olympics)	
9th	1928	Amsterdam	U.S.A.
10th	1932	Los Angeles	U.S.A.
11th	1936	Berlin	Germany
	1940	None — W.W.II	
	1944	None — W.W.II	
12th	1948	London	U.S.A.
13th	1952	Helsinki	U.S.A.
14th	1956	Melbourne	U.S.S.R.
15th	1960	Rome	U.S.S.R.
16th	1964	Tokyo	———

GLOSSARY OF GREEK WORDS

ALTIS—(Ahl-tis)—Sanctuary of Zeus at Olympia

ARETE—(Ah-réh-teh)—Perfection; of the highest quality

AIDOS—(Ay-dose)—Sportsmanship; of high moral character

BOULEUTERION — (Boo-lyou-téar-ee-on) — Council House of Judges and officials at Olympia

CAESTUS—(Kés-tus)—Boxing gloves of heavy leather thongs bound around lead or iron weights

DIAULOS—(Die-oh-loss)—400-yard dash in racing

DISKOBOLOS—(Dis-cob-oh-loss)—Discus thrower

DOLICHOS — (Doh-le-kos) — Three-mile, long-distance race

EPHEBOI—(Ehf-eh-boy)—That group of young Greeks made up of boys seventeen to nineteen years of age

EPINIKIA—(Eh-pea-knée-kee-ah)—An ode, a poem written in honor of an Olympic victor

HALTERES—(Hall-téar-eez)—Weights carried in hands of men when performing standing or running broad jump.

HIMATION—(High-máy-shion)—Flowing robe worn by Greek men and boys

HOPLITES—(Hop-lights)—Heavily armed infantry soldier; helmet, shield, breastplate, greaves

HORTHAY PALAY—(Hor-tháy páh-lay)—Free-for-all style of wrestling on the ground; contrasted with *kulisis*

KALOS K'AGATHOS—(Kah-lóws Kah-gah-thóss)— Beautiful and good

KALOS PAIS—(Kah-lóws pah-eés)—"The boy is beautiful"

KULISIS—(Koo-lée-sees)—Official, stand-up style of wrestling

PAIDOTRIBES—(Pie-do-treé-bes)—Athletic trainers

PANKRATION — (Pan-kráy-shee-on) — Brutal combination of wrestling and boxing; no holds barred

PELOPONNESE—(Péll-oh-poh-néese)—Southern half of Greece, the ancient realm of Pelops; means "Pelops' island"

PRYTANEIS—(Príh-ta-nees)—Olympic priests

PRYTANEION—(Prih-táy-knee-on)—Council house and residence of priests

PENTATHLON—(Pen-táth-lon)—Five events in which all contestants compete in running, jumping, wrestling, discus javelin throwing

PENTATHLETE—(Pen-táth-leet)—Man who participates in *pentathlon*

SPONDOPHORES—(Spon-dah-four-eeze)—Heralds who went throughout Greece to proclaim the Olympic truce and announce dates set for Olympic games.

STADE—(Stáy-d)—Race; the 200-yard dash

TAVERNAS—(Tah-vér-nas)—Inexpensive restaurant

XAIRETE — (Khé-reh-teh) — Rejoice, Be Happy (A greeting)

INDEX